Discovering Intention:

A Sensitive's Guide to the

Engineering Mind

Jeffrey P. Carpenter

To CECILIA: TRUST YOUR PATH,
EMBRACE YOUR VISION,
FIND YOUR INTENTION!

Discovering Intention: A Sensitive's Guide to the Engineering Mind

Copyright © 2015 by Jeffrey P. Carpenter.

ISBN-13: 978-1511803564
ISBN-10: 1511803568

Contents

This book is dedicated to all of the people who have supported me throughout this journey that I have taken. The trust that I have received from those who have helped me to explore my new sensitivity has been incredible, and I could not have achieved what I have without it.

 I would like to especially thank my family for sharing their enthusiasm and passions with me, encouraging me every step of the way during the writing of this book.

Chapter 1: Introduction

"Here we go again..." How many friends have brought this kind of groan out of you because of their stubbornness or shortsighted resistance toward facing a recurring personality issue they have? And on how many occasions? You have an important person in your life, whom you care about dearly, yet the person just can't get himself to face the fact that he has a "blind spot," caused by some challenging habit or character trait. As good friends often do, you grudgingly accept the situation, yet you try to find different ways to help your friend see other options, other behaviors, even other flaws he himself has pointed out in other people, in the hopes that he can at least try to admit that he needs to tackle this challenging behavior head-on. With this acknowledgement, you are certain he can truly attempt to address his own issues. Self-awareness cannot be forced upon another person, yet you know that only your friend can fix himself. You put up with the problem while continuing to gently, or not so gently, help your friend to see the error of his ways.

At least, this is what I *hope* my "friend" was thinking about me when he uttered that same four-word mantra of his for at least the twentieth time due to my never-ending questioning: "But HOW does this work?!" To this day, I still haven't mastered seeing through his humor-laden sarcasm that is sharper than even my own. His unrelenting attacks on my logical thought process always seem to make sense at the time. It is only later, as I think about it, that I recognize how he tends to give me just enough analytical evidence to push me in the "right" direction (i.e., HIS direction) without really answering the original question I asked. Then again, since my friend is an 800-pound, jet-black panther with emerald-green eyes who presented himself as my Spirit Guide during my first day of Reiki training, it's kind of hard to read his facial expressions.

The scope and depth of Reiki (pronounced "ray-key") are the subjects of many books and instructional classes, and I will be exploring my exposure to both the esoteric science and the physics approaches to Reiki healing. For my purposes, Reiki is the channeling of energy with the intention to provide physical and emotional healing. The metaphysical aspects include the Reiki practitioner becoming a conduit to draw energy from a healing plane and guide it into the subject to address specific ailments, or even to allow the energy itself to flow to where it is needed. Working with energy centers, called chakras, the healer directs energy and helps to remove emotional and physical "blockages" found in the equilibrium of the recipient. On the side of physics, matter and energy are directly related in the human body. With examples like electrical impulses controlling movement of the body's muscles, the autonomous nervous system driving the heart and lungs, and the results of magnetic resonance imaging (MRI) showing illness and physical damage throughout the body, it can be demonstrated that energies at varying frequencies flow through us all. Medicinal treatments using vibrations and pulses to soothe sore muscles and promote better blood flow continue to grow in popularity. In spite of this and other supporting evidence, many of us, me included, have struggled with accepting the connection between Reiki and modern medicine, not to mention those between natural and paranormal energy. When starting a new journey of enlightenment, knowing the path and walking the path are two very different things. Following a giant black panther down the path? That is another story altogether...

My first steps down this unexpected path of energy exploration were due to a physical event that I was looking to explain. On the recommendation of a friend, I took part in a Reiki class in the hopes that the Reiki master would help me understand a new-found ability to generate heat energy from my hands; being able to channel soothing heat out of your palms is great for massaging sore muscles and even for warming up your blankets on a chilly evening, and the class held the possibility for me to learn how to control it more effectively. Let's just say I was ill-equipped for the change I would go through after those several hours of Reiki instruction on that windy Saturday afternoon. Regardless of the manner in which you first experience this kind of personal upheaval, it can truly shake the roots of your being and make you question your self-definition...and that can be a good thing. I must add here that I can only hope you have the kind of friend that I had supporting me during these trying times. With as frustrating as our debates have been, I could not have wished for a better guide than my incorporeal panther mentor. I am compelled to thank him profusely for all of his patience and direction...also because he just appeared over my right shoulder and "reminded" me that I didn't do this alone. (He certainly isn't shy...)

For a person who has lived his entire life looking at the world through a "lens" of logic, I decided early in my childhood that an education based upon engineering disciplines would determine my career path. The personal satisfaction I derive from understanding why things work, how forces interact, and how to solve various technical problems is rewarding. I have even found a certain spiritual base in this grounded approach to life through my ability to analyze events, situations, and even relationships. But if I force myself to identify a "blind spot" in my analytical methods, I must admit that accepting this spiritual evolution that I continue to live through has been one of the most challenging things that I have ever dealt with. I know it is all due to my desire to understand the "why" of the experiences, as I seek to confirm to myself that these experiences have been real and are not just part of my active imagination. You see, the important point above all is that to accept these phenomena, I need to demonstrate to myself that they are happening outside of me as external events.

Yet Reiki was only the first step into this realm of energy sensitivity. I am still surprised at where my spiritual evolution has taken me, and there continue to be moments of fear and doubt that derive from that consuming need to analyze the reasons why these events and changes are taking place. This unexpected connection with reading and guiding energy made me want to learn more and experience more. I immersed myself in the natural energy of vortexes emanating up from the earth. The success of these experiments led me down a new road of discovery through the study of paranormal energy. When I heard that sensitivity to the paranormal is often the "natural progression" of a practicing energy healer, I thought it was a pretty unusual perspective to have, but I can't argue, now that it makes more sense to me. Research and practical experimentation with techniques for developing myself as a medium have expanded my sensitivity, and I try to schedule regular paranormal investigations to "practice" what I have learned. The scientist in me will not give up on trying to find rational explanations for the visions and experiences I have, and I feel I am a stronger sensitive for it. I am still learning the signs and indicators of spiritual communication that interact with my own energy. I am hoping that my second Spirit Guide, a quiet, unassuming faceless monk named Ezekiel, can help me bridge the gap between sensitivity and mediumship with the entities that continue to try to communicate with me.

Taking you on my journey of spiritual growth, I will share some insights on the obstacles I faced, the emotional trauma I lived through, and the rewards and enlightenment I received after going through these challenges to my beliefs and my habits. (To this day, I still experience an ironic twinge of uncertainty telling people that a giant black panther appears next to me and bosses me around, but he is still patient with me...most times, anyway. Ezekiel silently waits by my side until I ask him a question, so I think I have to work with him more to loosen him up.) While I will describe my experiences and practices in some detail, the journey is not intended to be an instructional manual on how to proceed with learning Reiki healing or to develop your own sensitivity. There are many good sources available that can help anyone move forward in these pursuits. What I do want to share will show you that you never know when you may be faced with a strange and inexplicable shift in your life's direction, and you can be your own best guide on how you assimilate these new truths into your current existence. If you feel a certain level of fascination as you review the inner workings of my transformation, you might want to look into helping your own change along and test yourself.

Let me give you a few examples of what I am talking about. They might help explain the radical shift in my life's paradigms and show how someone like me might get around to accepting these new sensitivities. My Reiki training was based on understanding the principles used in the channeling of universal healing energy, but as with everything else you learn, you have to find out for yourself how effective you are at it. I will explain in later chapters how visions and other mental messages come to me, but I want to give you a hint of what you have in store for you. Upon returning to work after one of my weekend paranormal trips to Tombstone, Arizona (and just wait until you hear about THOSE experiences), I was telling a co-worker who wasn't aware of my new sensitivity about my energy healing visions. He was a skeptic about all of this "crazy vision stuff," but the descriptions I gave him intrigued him to the point of challenging me: "Then prove it," he said with a smirk on his face. "Can you read me?"

It was like he gave me "permission" to examine him, opening up my Reiki sensitivity to connect to his energy. I could see that he was suffering with a strained back by a telltale red "slash" of pain in his energy. At first, he denied it, but then he said, "Wait, oh yeah, I did hurt my back while working on my house this weekend." His smirk turned into a grin when he asked, "What else?" I resumed my now-practiced energy scanning, and I saw that his energy aura had a red glow around his knee. He confirmed that he had injured it; it was aching that day in relation to a humidity change in the weather. In my mind's eye, I stripped away the physical "layer" of his energy aura to examine the mental and emotional layer that, for me, is beneath it. As an aside, I have no idea how these energy levels are represented for other Reiki healers, but all of my descriptions I will give you will come from the perspectives that I formed about my own experiences. I took a moment to examine him up and down his body. I could see knotted black energy in his gut (known as the Solar Plexus chakra) and a roiling, viscous negative energy in his chest (in the Heart chakra). As I looked deeper, I saw a dark line of energy connect the two points. Peering "into" this negative connection between the two chakras, a brief movie-like scene came to mind: a mountain villa with some well-tended gardens as well as farm animals in front of it. The vision shifted to people I didn't know arguing with my co-worker over this property, and I received intuitive hunches that these were part of his extended family. I let my perception shift back to normal, and I said to him, "You are upset and struggling with some personal issue with land and a property outside of the US. Your family is mad at you, thinking that you are making a decision that they deserve to be a part of. Are you looking to sell this family land?" In fairness to the story, I have to admit that I knew that his family had extensive acreage in Europe; he had mentioned it several months earlier. I had no idea about the financial situation, though, and we had never talked about that land again. He looked at me, his smile growing wider with his surprise, and he said, "I'm planning on selling that land I told you about. Things are changing in the family, and dealing with international land maintenance is gonna be tough. But how the hell do YOU know that!?" I looked at him, shrugged, and said, "I just saw all of that when I read you." He shook his head and laughed. His eyes went wider as he said, "This is freaking me out...I'm gettin' outta here." He walked back to his desk, turned off his computer, packed up his belongings, and left for the day. I saw him again a few days later when we were both in the office again, and he was fine; he just couldn't believe what I had told him.

Another example comes from my interest in the paranormal. My energy sensitivity has evolved, and I am working to improve my ability to "tune into" paranormal energies. The stories of the things I've witnessed are just as crazy as the Reiki visions I receive, and many of these events were experienced by those around me as well. During one of my mother's visits to the East Coast, we decided to take a few tours of allegedly haunted locations to see what we might find. The first stop was at the Burlington County Prison Museum[1]. I had been there before, but it was her first visit to the small, well-preserved museum. As we are walking around the prison's ground floor, we headed over to the east wing. There were a few small cells with bulky gates in a hall that ended at a storage room. In this small room were several displays made by children, as if the prison had hosted a children's craft fair. There were hand-made toys, dioramas, and puppets that showed different settings in an elementary school. One of the dioramas on the far end of the chamber was turned away from us. My mother stepped around the other displays on the floor to see what it showed. It was a cute shadow box of a mock school room, complete with chalk, mini blackboard, and lesson books. When she came back across the room, I made my way over to look at it myself. I asked her if she had seen the stuffed giraffe in the display, but she hadn't, so she went back to look again. Upon her return, she stopped for a moment and started to wipe her forehead and face with her fingers; she was searching for something that she had felt. She came over to me, leaning forward, and said, "Is there a cobweb on me? I can't find it." I looked and saw nothing...but then I remembered previous experiences I had in this prison. As I looked up to tell her this, she had just had the same thought: "Wait! This is what you told me about your last trip here - the cobwebs all over the place!" I just smiled and said, "See?" It's important to note that we had just walked through this path between the toys five times without feeling anything. The room was clean and dry and relatively dust-free. On the sixth trip, she felt like she walked into a sticky cobweb that clung to her as she walked forward. When I walked down the path again, I felt a sticky substance against my left thigh, below the leg of my shorts, and I couldn't find any explanation for it. We took some pictures and tried to reproduce the experience that we had shared, but we found nothing. Finally, we decided to move on with our tour. She proceeded through the doorway, but when I stepped through, I felt a wave of static hit me. The area in front of my face had gotten cold, to the point that I could actually see the steam of my breath. I developed this dizzy feeling, and I felt a type of contact at the edge of my personal energy field. Had some entity just tried to communicate with me? We were pretty excited by the activity in the prison, and it charged us up for the rest of the day of ghost hunting.

How can I explain all of this? Time and time again, I have experienced some pretty fantastic events. As an engineer, I would love to tell you that it has been a straightforward timeline of theory, training, analysis, and implementation in my exploration of these abilities. The truth is I have been my own biggest obstacle, but not in the sense of preventing me from seeing or reading energy; that would have been too straightforward. I could see amazing energies, wondrous visions, and I was validating the practical aspects of the experimentation, collecting results through the repetition of a specific set of procedures. My problem was accepting what I witnessed as visions from some external source, rather than something I created myself. The early symbolism was difficult to understand, and the glimpses of visions were easily explained away as simply the product of an active mind. But were they just figments of my imagination? Then, when I least expected it, it happened; I experienced a Reiki vision that I never could have made up, relaying to me information that I never even knew in the first place...and it shattered my doubts and made me really start probing the symbols I received in the future. Letting go of some of that early resistance opened even more doors to new sensitivity levels, ones I am still exploring. I selected some of these new doors myself, and I look forward to finding out what is on the other side of them.

One of the most grounding ideas to me about Reiki is that anyone can do it. Anyone can embrace these intangible assets of intention, healing, sight, and energy that Reiki helps us engage. The logic of intentional thought drives the pursuits, and you may be surprised at where you are led. Accepting the theory that energy cannot be destroyed but simply changes form, think about the possibilities. I never expected that understanding energy through Reiki would develop into sensitivity to other forms of energy, both natural and supernatural, and I bring the same levels of analytical skepticism I used with Reiki to bear on these new experiences. With my paranormal sensitivity developing out of the blue, it drove me to try and understand those energies better, so - and telling people this can still bring a smirk to my face - I wanted to become a spirit medium. The experiences I have are all the more real to me because of my search for proof and validation that they are truly external events, rather than things I've imagined. As I tell my stories, it seems like there is a theme to the response I usually get. After I share a story, the listener will often say, "Whoa, that is crazy!" to which I usually reply, "YOU think it's crazy? How do you think *I* feel?!" The people who know me well tell me that they give that much more credence to my experiences because they know that I take the time to question and validate each and every event. They know my engineering mind drives my evaluation of this new spirituality. If, after I challenge the phenomena, I still believe in what has happened to me, then there is probably something there after all.

As I started the process of illuminating my evolution of metaphysical energy sensitivity, I had a curious notion that there have been many different components of my life mixing together like ingredients in some bizarre recipe that I am still writing myself. Start with a communications engineer, trained in aerospace engineering, with an interest in the afterlife. Mix in one part of heat channeling through his hands. Add two parts of Reiki Practitioner certifications. Stir slowly, and watch the engineer question every intangible experience that happens, especially those that are confirmed by Reiki clients as being "real." Let sit for a few months, as the newly developed Reiki practitioner goes out into the world and gathers experiences, arguing more and more frequently with a certain smart-assed panther that no one else can see. When the Reiki engineer starts accepting the results of his healing using a minimum of evidential proof, quickly bring things to a boil, overwhelming him with the idea that he is a budding sensitive, moving beyond intention-driven energy healing and into the paranormal. As the engineer begins to explore this new adaptation to energy sensitivity, introduce a second Spirit Guide for the realm of spirit mediumship, showing himself as a Jesuit monk in charcoal gray robes and an almost incandescent white rope belt. How do you think THIS recipe turns out? I will let you know; the reviews are still rolling in, but I can describe how things have come together so far. Maybe it's a recipe you will see as worthwhile to test out for yourself...

Chapter 2: Origins

Using Reiki as a starting point, the concepts of Reiki have existed for a long time, but the story of its re-emergence was spread by its first attuned Western master, Hawayo Takata. The training sessions she hosted in her schools in Hawaii included the accounts of Reiki's rediscovery, attributed to Dr. Mikao Usui. Dr. Usui was reportedly a teacher in a Catholic school in Kyoto, Japan. One day, his students tested the teachings he provided by asking him to perform a miracle in order to prove the words of the Bible as literal truth. When he was unable to comply, he decided to seek out a stronger spiritual connection like the ones he had read about in the scriptures. He left the school and began a pilgrimage to find enlightenment. He expanded his studies to other religions, and in the Buddhist sutras written in their original Sanskrit, he found what he was sought: the various symbols of healing now used in the practice today. Realizing that he needed to find a way to tap into the power of the symbols, he traveled from his monastery home to climb a nearby mountain, seeking wisdom on the use of the symbols. On his way to the mountain, he collected a pile of 21 stones to keep track of the days he planned to spend on the mountain; at the beginning of the new day, he would throw one off of the mountain. He fasted and meditated religiously each day, but the days went by uneventfully. After a few weeks, he began to feel that all of his meditation was for naught. (Believe me, I know EXACTLY how he felt, sitting there and waiting for something to happen, and then nothing!)

On the last day, just after he tossed the final pebble off of the mountain, a light appeared off in the distance. It sped directly toward him, striking him in the middle of his forehead, his Third-Eye chakra. He began to see bubbles in the intensely bright light, four in all, each with one of the four Reiki symbols representing the levels of attunement within the study of Usui Reiki healing. He received instruction on the use of and the healing techniques associated with each of the symbols. During his journey back to the monastery, he performed three miracles of healing on people he had met. Upon his return home, he shared his new gift with anyone who wished to learn, and the wisdom he obtained began to spread.

With this background in mind, I would like to introduce you to my Spirit Guide of Reiki healing, the Panther. Yes, that is the name I use for him: "the Panther." He still hasn't given me an actual name, after all this time, and I have wondered if this is significant for one reason or another. To him, it doesn't seem to matter at all. When we communicate with each other, we don't need names, and it's not like I am dealing with a whole *litter* of gigantic black panthers running around me; then again, if there were, my opinions on all of this might be *very* different. He isn't my only Spirit Guide, though, and I will discuss my second Spirit Guide later. For a long time, I wasn't aware that I might have multiple Guides helping me and imparting wisdom. The Panther, being the first and having to deal with my initial confusion, had to bear the brunt of my analytical doubts while directing my healing training.

The Panther came to me; I did not summon him. I didn't even realize what was going on until later. I do need to point out that, for me, his "appearance" and our first interactions defined my approach to Reiki, and to the paranormal, going forward. The symbols and events I receive that I possess no prior knowledge about are the most important indicators that they are coming from some source outside of me.

It all started in a small séance chamber of a leased office where the Reiki class was being held. The fact that it was called a séance chamber didn't help me to take things any more seriously. I had joined the class for my own reasons, and I wanted to skim through the information and get to the practice sessions quickly. The Reiki master opened the class with a definition of the Usui System of Natural Energy, the particular school of Reiki we were to explore. I wasn't really committed to delving into all of the theory, but the Reiki master made the learning of the required symbols and the hand positions bearable. I struggled with believing in the reality of guiding intangible energy from another plane of existence, let alone channeling it into another person. In the initial training, however, one word opened my mind to a main principle of Reiki that provided clarity and insight. The word was "intention" - the intention to read another person's energy, the intention to be an energy conduit, the intention to heal. I started to understand that it was not random; it was controlled, similar to the feasibility of mind over matter. This is part of the foundation upon which my evolution has been built, and intention will be one of the main themes of my story. I will discuss more on intention later, but at this point, the Reiki master set up an exercise for the students to meet their Spirit Guides, and I almost laughed at how foolish it made me feel to go through the motions.

The master was playing a meditation bowl, filling the room with a metallic ringing sound and asking us to sink into a meditation. The opening instructions were to imagine ourselves in a beautiful landscape, a breezy mountain plateau covered in lush, rippling waves of grass. On the plateau, we were to construct a special garden for ourselves, and I had a nice mental image on what I wanted. There was a series of stone slabs in the earth, making a natural patio, and I had a high, almost overgrown garden of a variety of shrubs, plants, and exotic flowers. From outside of my meditative state, the Reiki master told us to make the garden our own, so my imagination went to work, creating a pool of koi surrounded by a stone wall, along with an antique-looking cast-iron bench for my sitting pleasure. I was feeling pretty good about my mental garden until I sensed something out of place. I felt the sensation of a significant weight pressing down on my left thigh. It actually brought me far enough out of my meditation to open one eye and look down at my lap, but nothing was there. I immediately slipped back into my meditation, and I was dumbfounded by the sight of an enormous feline head resting comfortably on my leg. The animal was almost obsidian in color, nearly the size of a young polar bear and sprawled out on the ground at my feet. The shock of seeing this panther in my fantasy garden impacted me even more when it opened its eyes and looked at me with disinterest, its emerald-green orbs reflecting the sun of my made-up world. (It was still an "it" at this point.)

I didn't have the time to consider the panther's appearance, because the Reiki master instructed the students to personalize the garden to make it our special place, and I wanted to pet a grizzly bear while sitting on my bench. I formed the shape of a bear in my mind and began to summon it several yards behind the bench. The panther slowly lifted its head from my lap and looked into my eyes. Voiceless, it sighed almost sarcastically and said, "I can do this all day, ya know..." It stood up, swung its right paw in the direction of the bear, and the image of the bear dissipated and vanished.

What the...? Instead of asking myself why a panther was even in my "dream," I chose to show that I was still in control of myself, summoning a big gray wolf into my garden. The wolf was on the other side of the koi pool, and it was striding toward me. I could sense a certain connection with the wolf that I cannot explain, but apparently, this connection meant nothing to this giant black "intruder" lying at my feet. The panther stood up again, shook its huge head, looked me in the eyes, and "spoke" again: "Wow...they told me you were smart; I'm not seeing it..." It raised its huge paw, swiped at the air in the direction of the wolf, and the wolf was no more. This was getting a little frustrating now. I looked at the huge black cat and said, in my meditation state: "What are you doing?!" The panther gave me that bored yet sarcastic look that I have grown to enjoy seeing and just laid down at my feet. I think it was watching the koi in the pool, but I can't be sure.

The Reiki master then asked the class to look off into the distance, maybe to the horizon of the plateau. She instructed us to actively invite our new Spirit Guide to come join us in the garden. With my formidable imagination, I had a plan to summon this Dark Ages-looking, robed wizard in long gray robes and a gnarled staff to join me. The tall, misty form began to materialize at the edge of the plateau, and I was looking forward to meeting him...until the panther raised its head from its paws and rolled its eyes, saying, "Ugh...we have a LOT of work to do..." It stood up, walked around the bench, and it glanced at the semi-solid wizard with disdain. Then it simply lifted a paw, extended its claws, and slashed them in the direction of the far-distant figure, and the figure dissolved into nothing, drifting away as a mist in the wind. The panther came back in front of me and stared into my eyes for a moment. Finally, it said, "...I'm already here." The panther walked out of my garden and then vanished. Nothing I did called it back. I was thoroughly confused, but before I could consider things further, the Reiki master ceased "playing" the meditation bowl, and my vision was gone. I was disappointed that I didn't get to meet my Spirit Guide.

With the meditation over, the Reiki master then started to describe possible forms of the Spirit Guides that people in the past have met. She discussed men, women, relatives who has passed, even pure energy. Some people even associate their healing skills with Power Animals. When she said this, the first of several body-quivering chills of TRUTH shook me down to my core, and I said under my breath, "You gotta be KIDDING me..." The Reiki master heard me utter this, and she asked, "Wait, what happened?"

Before I go on, it would probably help to provide some insight into my personality and beliefs. Understanding your perspective when you start a journey usually helps to explain some of the problems and choices along the way. It doesn't always explain why I would continue to reject the same conclusion over and over - and OVER - in the face of detailed and varying evidence, but maybe I am just gifted that way. Looking back at the early days, I would consider myself the last person I ever would have expected to go through a spiritual metamorphosis, particularly because I believe I know myself very well and know - or thought I knew - my capacity and capabilities. I have always been interested in science and engineering, and the analytic thought processes suit me well in my everyday life. Interestingly enough, I also thought about practicing law at one point, taking advantage of my ability to argue logically to my own end, but I chose to learn more about the physical laws of the world around me. This is not exactly a foundation for an excursion into the study of healing based on directed thought and intention. However, I do recognize a few traits in my personality that would make me open to trying to bridge the gap in some ways.

I am also aware that religious beliefs vary so greatly that it is often challenging to have impartial discussions about one person's beliefs without sparking debates. My religious code does include my belief in a Supreme Being - or God Source, as I have seen it labeled during my studies - along with life after death. But describing my own beliefs is not the purpose behind raising my point about religion. My point is more focused on a religious practice that almost every person is aware of: prayer. Whether or not you choose to pray is entirely up to you, but prayer does have something in common with Reiki from the perspective of its goals. Consider the example of a group of people coming together and offering prayers for some person's health. The group of people has the same goal in mind, and their individual investment in the process is simply their time...and their intention. The group joins their intentions together with the goal of healing their congregation member. Reiki uses intention for the same purpose; it uses different "tools" and processes, but both practices are driven by the intent to help another.

When dealing with people or issues, I take a certain pride in my ability to listen to both sides of an argument, and I have often used this to my benefit in order to reinforce my own opinions and beliefs. When I can have an open (well, open "enough," anyway) debate about two sides of an issue, and the outcome is that I still have the same opinions and perspective, it reinforces my belief and commitment to my point of view. It also leaves me with a sometimes problematic expectation of being able to find a rational explanation for everything I deal with, but it does give me some leeway to question theories in a different light.

On another note, similar to some people's narrow-minded impression of a stereotypical nerd, I always loved the genre of medieval fantasy, with the magic and larger-than-life adventures providing hours of enjoyment. The avid reading and the countless hours of mentally exploring different fantasy worlds strengthened my imagination into a well-honed tool, but this can make the results of Reiki healing work that much harder to accept. Having a strong imagination is often an asset, but it can be difficult to differentiate what is imagined from what might be symbols or scenarios received from a heightened awareness of energy. When you can visualize fantasy monsters, magic spells, and alternate worlds, how can you determine that the images your client "shares" with you are not just in your head? You need empirical evidence and a logical analysis.

Put all of this together, and you can imagine how the weight of a large, furry head pressing down on my thigh would cause me quite a bit of confusion in a very short amount of time. How do I explain this feeling on my leg? This is all in my mind, right? I understand my mind can play tricks on me, and it can make me think I am feeling this weight...but hold on a second. I didn't imagine the gigantic head in my little "happy place." The panther was there without my conscious intervention. If this is my subconscious mind, what do I do now?

All of these colliding thoughts flashed through me in what felt like only a few seconds, and I surprised myself when I answered the Reiki master's question by saying, "Well, it seems that my Spirit Guide is a giant black panther with emerald-green eyes..." She said, "Really? That's cool!" She instructed us to call on our Spirit Guides to ask for a sign on how we will know they are helping us. For some reason, instead of asking how my panther would help me, I asked, "How will I know you are here?" Suddenly, for the first of many times to come, a huge black feline face appeared up close in my field of vision, and the emerald eyes flashed with a deep green light. I whispered out loud, "Whoa," and the panther smirked, nodded, and vanished.

The Panther and I both realized that this was a meaningful exchange; I chose to open myself to the possibility that there actually may be some truth to all of this Spirit Guide stuff. The class continued, and I had a new outlook on it. The appearance of the Panther completely altered my investment in this training class for Reiki attunement. I suddenly couldn't get enough of it, with the chakras, hand positions, symbols, and crystals all having a new level of meaning for me. The attunements to the crystals were private ceremonies in which the Reiki master joined my energy with hand-made stone crystals etched with gold representations of the Level II symbols: cho-ku-rei, the power symbol, and Level I; sei-hei-ki, the mental/emotional symbol; and hon-sha-ze-sho-nen, the distance/time symbol, both at Level II. (The fourth symbol is dai-ko-myo, the Master's symbol, but I have not yet decided to pursue this Reiki Level III attunement.) As I learned the meanings and uses of my new crystals, I had my first unexplained impulse, nagging at the edge of my consciousness. I was drawn to the distance symbol. It is, by far, the most complex to draw and visualize, but to me, it became the most important, without really knowing why until later. There was an unanticipated power in the symbol, one that made itself known to me before I understood it. During the weeks after the class, I explored this power and realized it was the ability to channel healing across great distances and back and forth through the life of the recipient. I was already comfortable with the ideas of guiding healing light for physical and emotional healing; these were all driven by my intention. Distance healing and timeline reading were to become the strengths of my Reiki abilities.

My interpretation of a person's chakras is a bit of an adaptation. I always use the standard definitions of the chakras and their locations and purposes, but I visualize them a little differently than others do. Since this concept of chakras may not be "standard" to many people, I wanted to provide a quick summary of these energy centers. The individual chakras help to regulate the body's energy balances, and the energy within them spins freely when the person is healthy. Negative energy in the form of bad feelings or emotional "baggage" impairs the chakra's ability to spin, impacting its ability to support the body's well-being. There is also recent scientific research that can map some of these energy nodes in the human body, showing a collection of energy at specific points. The common locations of the major chakras are as follows, from top to bottom in the body:

- Crown chakra (top of the head)

- Third-Eye chakra (center of the middle of the brow)

- Throat chakra (middle of the neck)

- Heart chakra (heart area in the chest)

- Solar Plexus or Gut chakra (base of the torso, at the navel)

- Sacral chakra (pelvis area and the reproductive glands)

- Root chakra (bottom of the spine, the coccyx)

There are many interpretations of what these chakras "look" like, but my selection of imagery is that of a lens aperture on an old 35-mm film camera. The overlapping shutter pieces open and close the chakra as needed. In my engineering mind, the mechanical nature of the shutter allows for more direct "control" of the chakras, beyond what I would expect if I were to use some of the standard interpretations of a blooming Lotus flower. My ability to open and close my own chakras was one of the simpler things I mastered. Opening and cleansing my own chakras helps me to release my own negative energy before beginning my energy readings on my subject. (You may be wondering why I have been using words like "recipient" and "subject," instead of "person," while describing who is receiving my healing. I will be highlighting my Reiki readings and healing on animals in a later chapter, so I want to be clear that my clients have been more than just human beings. With a massive panther healing guide, there is a certain expectation placed upon me that I spread the healing around to the animal kingdom.)

Returning to my first Reiki training experiences, I continued to have flashes of insight, similar to the one I had with my affinity to the distance symbol, that I couldn't explain. The second unexpected impulse, and certainly not the last, pulled at my senses when the practical exercises began. The Reiki master had the students pair up and perform our first readings. In my pairing, I let my partner go first as the healer, and she went through the rituals of opening her chakras and reading my energy levels. She started by using a pendulum, analyzing the rotation of the crystal as a representation of the energy flow through my chakras. She focused often on my Throat chakra, saying it was somewhat closed but never telling me if she could see why. When we switched places, she asked to put a blindfold on to help her relax. Standing next to the table, leaning over her, I raised my hands to lay them on her shoulders for my first reading, but something nagged me at the edge of my mind, so I stopped. A stream of perceptions and thoughts flashed through my mind, and I picked up the pendulum myself. I described what I was doing while I was checking the state of her chakras, and then I put the device down.

Accepting the meaning of these flashes of images that came to me, I decided not to use the laying hands techniques. Instead, I closed my eyes and began to perform sweeping hand motions about 18 inches above her body. I was reaching out with my sensitivity rather than using the "laying of hands" technique that is the common practice. My shift in perception happened gradually, as I started to see different levels of light and dark gray energy flowing through her. You can imagine my surprise when I saw these bands of gray energy in my mind and was able to manipulate them in some way. I had to open my eyes several times to check if this energy was visible, but I could only see it in my mind's eye. Without warning, I saw an emotional cord leading up from her Heart chakra to her Throat chakra. A rush of symbols entered my mind, and I saw her attachment to an old woman. Putting all of these messages together into a single interpretation, I asked her why she was upset with her grandmother. She stopped breathing for a moment and slowly lifted the blindfold from her eyes, looking at me questioningly. "How did you know that?" I just shrugged. She reapplied the blindfold, and this time I told her I was going to touch her, but in only two places: on her Crown chakra at the top of her head and on her feet as a grounding mechanism. I decided to try and draw some of the emotional negativity, the dark gray energy circling in her Heart chakra, out of her by guiding it down her body to "pull" it out of her feet. I used my intention to visualize the draining of the dark mass from her torso and down to her right leg. When I saw it move down into her knee, it seemed to get stuck for some reason. At this very moment, she said, "I thought you weren't going to touch me. Do you see something in my knee? I feel your hand..." I said, "Take off the blindfold; I am at least two feet away from you..." She tore it off quickly, and I was standing toward the foot of the examination table, my hands still raised in the air. (I think I was as freaked out as she was that her senses detected this at the same time as I was guiding this energy to that spot...) She sat up, and in my mind's eye, I saw the energy "stuck" in her knee was tied to her Heart, the negative bond being rebuilt as I worked to draw the energy out of her. Without knowing how I received this intuition, I told her, "You know, you don't have to feel guilty about your grandmother; she knows you love her." My partner then did something I never expected - she cried on the massage table. Tears appeared in the corners of her eyes, and she whispered softly, "Thank you." We ended our readings there.

The conclusion of the class was not too long after my reading. For the next few days, I practiced my chakra cleansing rituals and meditated in my metaphysical garden, yet the Panther didn't join me. I did try my hand at a few basic healing exercises on my friends and family, but I felt and saw no evidence that the healing was effective. I resorted to "asking" the healing energy to flow through the subject and decide on its own how best to help. But that wasn't good enough for my scientific approach for developing this new ability; I wanted to control it actively, not just assume it was going to work. During a subsequent Reiki session weeks later, I remembered that the class directed me to ask my Spirit Guide how I would know when it was helping me, so I decided to give this a try. I focused on the face of the Panther in my mind and mentally asked, "Help me find the places I should send my healing to?"

Immediately, the Panther's face floated down from my Third-Eye chakra and over my subject, moving slowly from head to toe, pausing in certain locations on the body and emanating pulses of green light from its shining green eyes. I was seeing the healing pressure points through the Panther's eyes, watching the client's energy ebb and flow and even coagulate in the heart, legs, and throat zones. The view of white energy started to mix with what resembled a dark gray sludge or oil of emotional blockage. With the index finger of my right hand, I drew the emotion symbol in the air in front of me. Holding it in place mentally, I reached out and envisioned myself grasping the symbol, collecting the power of the symbol into my palm and then directing it to the Heart chakra first. The sludge was resilient; it changed shape and resisted my attempts to thin it out. Finally, I tried a different approach. Using the rotational flow of the chakra itself, I drove my intention toward spinning the viscous fluid in line with the person's own energy flow. Once the fluid was in motion, I started to drain it from the chakra itself and pull it through the torso down to the legs. In my healing work, the legs continue to be a workable "storage" place for the negative energy I pull from chakras and other locations, and the energy is then ready to be drawn out of the feet and discarded. I often "cast" it away once I pull it out of the feet so that it will not attach itself to me.

I realized relatively quickly that my engineering mind would need to break down and analyze the individual procedures and actions I performed; I'd need a set of repeatable steps to help me define and study this new facet of my life. There were too many new sensations, too many unexpected results. One of the things that kept me going, though, was that the Reiki work I did seemed to be helping the people I was practicing on. A friend once volunteered to let me test my Reiki training on her because she had been going through a series of sleepless nights. She lay down on her couch but couldn't seem to get comfortable. She was a bit nervous about what would happen during the Reiki session, but there was more to it than that. Later, she told me she was a little afraid of what I might tell her, since she had never done anything like this. I could only reassure her that I will tell her the truth about exactly what I saw. We got started, and immediately, I was shown images of red "splashes" of pain in her neck and shoulders, where she had pulled some muscles while exercising. By that time, I had learned enough about my personal Reiki process to continue reading her rather than starting to focus the healing energy on the physical issues; there were often emotional issues to be addressed first. I continued to scan her, and I was shown what I will describe as a thick, dark silt lingering in her Heart chakra, and there was this black "vein" of negative energy leading up through her torso to her Throat chakra. In her Throat chakra, a vision presented itself to me as a series of still pictures in my mind. (With my eyes closed, it still surprises me when these intuitions pop into my head, and it can take a few moments to interpret what I see.) I saw my friend when she was around 22 (another intuitive thought giving me her age), and she was having some type of argument with her sister. It was "obvious" from the empathic messages I received that the two sisters had never forgiven each other for whatever had happened between them. The next image was a family get-together, like an afternoon barbecue, and other family members were drawn into this heated argument. Part of my friend's emotional challenges was due to the fact that her sister continued to hold a grudge for all of these years, and my friend kept blaming herself. I opened my eyes and began to tell her what I had seen. Her eyes opened, and she smiled. Even though she was still carrying around that stress, she told me she felt better that someone else could "understand" what she was going through. I helped her clear out some of the negative energy that was causing her discomfort as well. She actually started to doze off toward the end of the session, which is a great indication of relaxation and stress relief. When I sat down again, she woke up, stretched, and sighed: "Wow...I wish you could do a session with my sister; she needs it..."

I wasn't always able to explain why I selected one Reiki technique over another, so my experimentation sometimes added to my confusion about how to proceed. Did I always have to stand over a person to read their energy? Was the actual power behind the Reiki energy readings the symbols I was drawing in the air with my fingers? These thoughts to analyze my Reiki practices came at a rather unexpected time: while I was mowing my lawn one Sunday afternoon. I have a good-sized yard, and I was about three-quarters of the way done when I thought about how mowing, like many repetitive activities of manual labor, can occupy the body while leaving the mind to think. Maybe I could perform distance healing during the hour or so it takes me to mow the lawn. I focused on a man struggling with hip problems that had really affected him, and my intent was to simply sending some relief. I started up the lawn mower again, turned it around, and guided it down the next diagonal cut in my back yard. First, I traced the image of the distance symbol in my mind, and then I drew the emotion symbol as I pushed the mower. My perception shifted a bit as I pushed, and a brief vision came to me. I was watching two brothers argue over something, inside an older building with all sorts of tools and materials around them. My "client" was pointing angrily at his older brother, and it seems this dispute was never resolved. The relationship was forever changed, and the man was full of regret. I tried to help relieve some of this guilt, but I had to stop and put more gas in the mower. Apparently, I didn't have to draw the Reiki symbols by hand; my intention and personal energy could infuse the mental images of the symbols with the energy needed to be effective. There was so much more to explore...

There were also times at which visions and insights came to me unexpectedly. While I can't predict when things might be shown to me, it took a long time to trust that I should act on these intuitions. I approached it from the perspective of what it would cost me to act on them: a little of my time and a bit of my own energy. But first, I had to recognize and acknowledge the visions I received; essentially, I had to figure out how to separate thoughts from "messages." There was a time when I set up an appointment to perform a Reiki session for a woman in her home. However, I was planning the session through a family member of hers, and the family member called the woman on a mobile phone to discuss an acceptable time. At one point during the phone call, I could see the woman's aura over the family member's left shoulder, with the cell phone against her left ear. When I agreed to the time, I was seeing gray nervousness in her aura remotely, and it took a moment to understand that I was seeing my future "client" as an emotional connection linking the family member to the woman. I was beginning to see how far intention might go for distance healing.

Once I identified the initial set of Reiki procedures and my own interpretations of symbols that provided satisfactory results, my evolution proceeded quickly. (Of course, it wasn't nearly this straightforward, but I will discuss how I had to break down my own walls of disbelief later.) I started receiving more images and insights from my Reiki readings than ever before. Each day, I added more and more people to my distance healing efforts...and why not? It required only my time and my wish to help the recipients. My intentions were twofold: to send the universe's healing energy to people and to practice this new ability and explore its effectiveness using scientific methods of experimentation. Therein lies the problem I struggled with for a long time. How could I prove that the effects of Reiki were real, when everything I have seen is in my mind? How can I learn more about making my healing stronger if I had no physical measurements to take and analyze? I wanted this power to be real, but I had no idea how I was going to test the effects. I had a very hard time believing that my instincts were true because I couldn't collect any hard evidence. The Panther would just say, "Why the heck does THAT matter? You're still missing the point..."

Before I begin recounting the early days of these spiritual changes that have made me redefine myself, I wanted to lay out some of the ground rules I will be following throughout the rest of the book. All of the revelations, visions, and encounters I will share from my Reiki sessions deal with the trials and emotional trauma of actual people. The descriptions of my experiences and my own feelings will be extensive and detailed, but I have chosen to respect the privacy and trust of the people involved by omitting their names and leaving out some of the specific details of their personal lives. My clients and the people who have asked for my help will know who they are when they read their stories, I have no doubt. The deconstruction of my experiences is sufficient to explain just how amazed I was while receiving these intuitive images and how hard it has been to accept that these experiences as true clairvoyant events. On most of the occasions, I wasn't even aware of the individual's past history leading up to my experiences, so leaving out the personal background of my "clients" shouldn't change the analysis of the process or the impact it had on both me and the subjects receiving the healing.

The descriptions of my surprise and frequent disbelief I have gone through are not intended as attempts to convince anyone of anything. There will be people who are open to learning more about what I will share, and there will be others who choose not to hear more. Finally, some people will dismiss all of it outright. I do thank those skeptics who have shown me the courtesy to blame someone else, rather than me, for "faking" some of the things I've observed. To me, this shows that at least they are respecting my integrity. I can assure you that every single story - every vision, every sensation and contact, all of it - actually happened to me. I am sure there are many people who will look for alternate explanations for the events that I will share, and I have always welcomed protests of incredulity and requests for factual evidence. Believe me, the need deep-down to prove the validity of these experiences has been, and continues to be, a huge part of my analysis of this evolution. I will be describing many of the internal dilemmas I faced while trying to reconcile two forces inside me: the scientific and the metaphysical. I have debated with myself the "reality" of these sensations and observations in every case, and it has strengthened my acceptance of the evolution and expanded my own personal investment. My sharing of the doubts, struggles, interpretations, and next steps is as much for me as it is for you. I encourage you to question everything you will read here. If even a single "unexplainable" event encourages you to rethink your perspectives, it will justify the journey.

Chapter 3: Analytical Debates

Maybe I spent too much time trying to analyze the inner workings of the Reiki effects, or maybe I didn't want to admit that I couldn't figure out how to analyze them. The good news is that the Reiki healing started to show results more frequently, and it became easier to summon. Unfortunately, the growing success also introduced more frustration and doubts about whether or not I was actually invoking it myself. For several months, I was consumed with identifying the specific energy properties that determined how the healing worked. The Panther faced a never-ending stream of questions from me, and he guided me forward without truly answering them, much to his own amusement. Instead of engaging in my debates on how the Reiki healing itself worked, he would appeal to my analytical mindset, using my own arguments against me around how my defined processes continued to show success. The Panther chose my commitment to perform impartial experimentation as the cornerstone of his responses; he skillfully urged me down the path of Reiki by focusing on its results rather than its inner workings. To my own credit, I still found a way to accept the wisdom he shared with me in spite of all of this frustration, but as I look back, I argued about almost everything:

- How do I determine which images were energy symbols and which were just random thoughts?

- Are my individual experiences during meditation and readings affected by my practices and methodology?

- Can I prove that the distance healing is successful if I never actually see the person?

- How do I know that the healing I direct at myself is effective?

- Is my standing above a person, walking back and forth next to him, the most effective way for me to read him?

- Why does any of this actually work???

Many of my questions can be related to a single point: What is the basic formula for Reiki? The techniques of energy healing are easy to find, but science has lagged far behind in empirically testing and validating the results. Many cultures have employed medical techniques such as acupuncture, qigong, tuina, and others for centuries. With all of the writings and teachings available for these methodologies, the analytical evaluation of the results of these practices is challenging at best. Conversely, scientific theories that have become immutable laws can be tested with documented procedures, and the test results are repeatable. Can we actually use the same principles to evaluate the medical effects of Reiki? Barring the medical examination that confirms the removal of the ailment, the measurable changes in Reiki are often thought to be too subjective to be considered effective. Is it "good enough" that the client says that he feels better?

In comparison, there are many fundamental principles in engineering that define the interaction of forces and can predict the effects of different variables. One of my favorites is the Bernoulli equation for fluid dynamics that measures the different pressures on an object depending upon the speed of the fluid flowing around it. Considering that air has similar properties as fluids when in motion, and the object is an airplane wing with a distinct camber (or curvature), there is a growing pressure differential on the wing as the air flows faster around it. Following Newton's Third Law of Motion, if the wing exerts force on the air, then the air must create an equal and opposite reaction force upon the wing[2], introducing the phenomenon of lift, the principle granting flight. At any given point on the wing, the pressure can be estimated, and changing the shape of the leading edge of the wing where the air first flows around it can improve the lift efficiency. An engineering formula can identify the impact of every wing design change and calculate an ideal airspeed to provide the appropriate lift for different payloads on the plane: $L=C_i(A\rho v^2)/2$, as shown on the cover, where L is the lift, C_i is the lift coefficient, A is the wing area, ρ is the air density, and v is the air speed over the wing[3].

Then there is Einstein's famous equation $E=mc^2$, part of his Theory of Relativity that is widely held as one of the most influential theories in both particle physics and universal energy exchange[4]. I can tell you that the Panther likes Einstein's theory, too, as it suits his needs. There are a few components in this suite of theories that illustrate ways in which people can learn to accept Reiki as a viable medical treatment. Einstein himself discussed how the elements of these theories were based upon empirical discovery and then evolved into mathematical representations later to predict future actions and reactions, which he described as principle theories rather than constructive theories[5]. The Panther could certainly argue that the results of Reiki can be measured by the discovery of their effects; to understand Reiki, the healer must understand the principles upon which it is based. The equation $E=mc^2$ itself can be an important theory to support Reiki's effectiveness. If energy and matter are equivalent, then energy is in all matter in some form. For example, the regeneration of cells in the human body can take place if energy can be transmuted into matter to strengthen cellular bonds and repair organ damage. Energy as fuel for cellular mitosis creates new cells within the muscles and tissues of the body, promoting restoration. With electrical impulses running through the body, improving the energy flow through cells can enhance mobility and regulation of the body's processes. All of this sounds logical and evidential, don't you think? It stands to reason that this kind of approach would have helped me understand my initial steps in my exploration of Reiki. Unfortunately, I never actually MADE any of these associations at the beginning of my Reiki training. Why would I?! Apparently, I had decided that would be much better to make it as frustrating as possible and learn the hard way! I know the Panther enjoyed this approach immensely.

During the early stages of practicing Reiki, it really helps to keep a journal. The initial challenges I faced were spread throughout every step of the process, and jotting down my experiences, feelings, and the associated client feedback created a record for future review. The development of a lexicon of symbolic Reiki messages can be slow at first, but my journal helped me put some of the meanings together. I would look at a client, staring intently at locations on the body where I believed the chakras would be, yet I saw nothing unusual. I scrutinized each chakra zone, inspected the arms and legs, and examined the neck and head with no visual indicators. As I took a break and decided to try and read the feet, I had to remind myself to focus; I couldn't let my imagination interrupt my diagnosis by making up that little white band of light on the shoulder. My inspection of the feet didn't prove any more fruitful, but now I felt like I was getting too distracted and not taking things seriously. I put that gray mass on the knee out of my mind and redoubled my efforts. I tried to go back to basics, laying my hands on the throat, but not feeling anything at all. Maybe I was tired, or my hand had fallen asleep; putting my hands on my hips in frustration, my fingers started to tingle, so I shook my fingers to increase the blood flow and got back to the investigation. When the client told me of the pains and other physical issues being experienced, I sent my thoughts to these spots one at a time and envisioned what the insides of the body part would look like. I had to rebuild my mental image of the knee joint several times because I kept seeing a dark jagged line in the cartilage, but I finally got it right. When I was done, I felt a little drained and disappointed at my lack of success, but I diligently wrote in my journal about how I hadn't seen anything of note and resorted to listening to the client to guide my selection of problems to address. I also jotted down that I need to rest more before a Reiki session, because I kept letting my mind distract me with unnecessary imagery. Do you see my mistakes yet? As much as I take pride in my attention to detail, I seemed to excel in explaining away some pretty important messages.

During the next Reiki session, I called on the Panther to help me identify the locations in physical distress. I envisioned the Panther looking over the client from the other side of the table, and his gaze would leave a lingering glow of green light floating above the person, so I would disregard my frustrating distraction of a charcoal-colored paste in the person's throat to send my thoughts to the Panther's selected spots. In a few cases, I actually had to remove my own random thoughts about a specific location on the body before I could zoom in on my view of the Panther's emerald markers. I'm sure you can imagine see how disappointed I was at my lack of improvement at identifying issues on my own. In retrospect, maybe the Panther should have just hit me over the head with an obvious direction, since I didn't seem to be getting the subtle messages being sent to me...

By now, you can also see that I didn't actually trust myself; it was only weeks later, after reviewing my journal, that I realized I was misinterpreting the symbols I was seeing. I was disregarding them as figments of my imagination or stray thoughts that I was having, yet these visual cues increased in frequency and length as I practiced. When I finally overcame my mental block to accepting my energy symbols, I relied on the Panther's eyes less and less to guide me during readings. However, I found other reasons to doubt the effectiveness of the healing and my evolving decisions on how to perform the sessions. He would still use offhand logic to alleviate my concerns, and he still wouldn't really answer me:

Me: "Whoa, I feel drained. The Reiki master said that she heard other practitioners say they can't handle more than three sessions in a day, because they got tired from adding their own energy."

Panther: "Yes."

Me: "Maybe that's what I am doing, even though I don't think I am doing it on purpose."

Panther: "Yes."

Me (becoming a bit agitated): "If I am putting my own energy into it, I should rethink this."

Panther: "Why would you do that?"

Me: "If I am giving too much of my own energy, I must not be doing it correctly."

Panther: "You're doing fine."

Me: "But the Reiki master said..."

Panther: (sighing for the hundredth time) "Look - are you going to turn this into a full-time job?"

Me: "Well, no...At least I don't plan on it."

Panther: "Does it work better when you put a little of yourself into it?"

Me: "Oh yes, it does. I feel more connected, and it seems I visualize much better when I..."

Panther: "Then what are you complaining about?! This is how you are connecting..."

Me: "Yeah, but how is it better if I am not doing it right?"

Panther: "Because I said so." (disappears)

Me: "All right, all right...sheesh..."

Panther: (a disembodied voice right next me) "I can still hear you; you DO realize that, right?"

Another debate I raised was around my choice of procedures and rituals to complete my energy readings. I continued to look for step-by-step procedures that I could replicate in order to "guarantee" success. To be honest, this was mostly a one-sided argument, because the Panther would rarely tell me what I was supposed to do during a Reiki reading with a client. He would simply say, "It's your intention; do whatever you want." I finally understood that he wasn't dismissing my question; he was reminding me that the healer's intention is the key to all Reiki work. After this realization, I let myself be led by the same intuitive messages that I received during visions. Much of my Reiki work in those early days was more challenging because my subject was often miles away, so my use of the distance symbol was frequent. I tried many different ways to drive my intention into different representations of the symbol, yet I settled on concentrating my focus by drawing it myself with my right forefinger. This procedure has evolved into my drawing the intricate, four-part distance symbol on an object near me, sometimes even using my leg as a "notepad." Once the drawing is complete, I direct my energy into the symbol as I manually collect all the parts into a fist in my right hand and then cast the energy into the air out in front of me, focusing on the image of the subject who will receive it. When I think I have attuned myself with the subject, I begin the energy reading.

Now, I don't want you to get the idea that all of my early Reiki exploration and activities were frustrating. There were many times when it was a lot of fun. I might have actually given up on it if I didn't find some kind of enjoyment in it, and the appreciation of my clients was rewarding. If nothing else, the Reiki session does relax and soothe the clients, and they usually have a great night's sleep after a full session. There were also a few turning points in my practice that gave me encouragement about my future experiences. One turning point reminded me of the impact of watching classic movies when the movie suddenly changes from black-and-white to color.

While working on a client, I was performing my usual energy scans, and I saw some negative energy in the form of a dull gray sludge in her Heart chakra. I tried drawing some of the sludge out of the chakra to move it down towards her legs and feet, but it was thick and hard to "grab." I decided to try something else and moved my scans to her Throat chakra. I noticed something above her throat. As I focused on it, I saw several gray, hazy lines leading up the outside of each side of her neck to several locations on each cheek. The intuitive messages I received told me that these lines were linking her continuing acne issues with her thyroid gland. I started sending my intention from her cheeks down through these "tubes" to her thyroid to work on the chemical imbalance I sensed. She would later tell me that it seemed to help her for a while. From here, I moved down to her stomach, as I had found a "slash" of pain on the left side of her abdomen. I gazed more deeply "into" her energy to see what appeared to be a scar or ulcer within her intestine. I directed energy through her digestive system to help heal this wound. Now that I was able to read her energy state, I thought I should go back and work on the blockage in her Heart chakra.

As I visualized lifting this paste out of her chakra to help normalize its natural spin, it would just slide through my fingers. I focused my determination to try a different approach to scooping this sludge out, and suddenly, a smooth, light-brown cream poured into her Heart chakra. It filled the chakra and began to churn in a counter-clockwise direction, as if being mixed and aerated by imaginary blades inside the heart. This made me laugh out loud for two reasons: 1) it had the consistency and texture of melted fine chocolate, and the intuitive messages told me for certain that it was a smooth, creamy chocolate; and 2) it was the first time I had ever seen something during a Reiki vision that was in color, rather than shades of gray or pulses of white. I had finally learned my lesson about disregarding symbols or messages during a Reiki session, so I said, "Ok, this HAS to be my imagination, but I have to ask: why am I seeing some light-brown chocolate filling up your heart?" The client's eyes sprung open. With a meek smirk, she responded: "Because I was just thinking about the Belgian chocolate I was going to eat when we were finished, and it made me happy?" I was shocked by this revelation, and the client and the friend she invited to watch the session were both staring at me in disbelief. This was incredible; I spent a lot of time trying to analyze how I saw that vision as soon as she started thinking about it. While reflecting upon this event during my journal update, I couldn't help but notice that this vision supported some of the theories behind Reiki that negative and positive thoughts can directly influence a person's well-being. (You might be thinking how obvious this is, saying, "Well, DUH! Chocolate makes EVERYTHING better!")

I cannot fully explain how, but this event also opened many doors for my future Reiki practices and treatments. After this event, my Reiki healing work had more "interactive" symbolism, in which I received more "feedback" from the client on how to direct my energy for better results. Future images were also colorized, including the telltale red "slashes" of pain that I often see without even focusing. I invested some time in studying pictures and diagrams of different parts of the body to use my new colorized images in a more specific way on a client's ailments; knowing more about what the body looks like from the inside helps me guide the energy to where it needs to be applied. Even the Panther was proud of me when the color started flowing in; he stood there smiling at me and teasing me at the same time, "What took you so long?"

That was pretty generous of him, because he was usually fending off my unending list of questions on how to measure everything from the effectiveness of my healing on a given recipient to the progress of the increasing strength of my Reiki abilities. Without having to focus and prepare myself, I would receive visions and intuitive messages about physical pains of people I knew and of complete strangers. I would even question the Panther about the range of my sensitivity, and he would just shrug. When I insisted on some kind of guidance, he said, "You can accept that you have been attuned to a crystal that allows you to send energy over long distances and even back and forth through time, but you can't figure the range out for yourself?" It didn't seem to matter to me that I had reached a point where I could read people when they put me on the spot to perform an unplanned Reiki analysis or even while they were walking down a hallway or into a restaurant. I kept looking for some way to compare my evolution to the "standard" way that a Reiki practitioner progressed in the use of his gift. (Insert the Panther rolling his eyes here.) Thinking about it now, it was a pretty foolish effort; I spent more time trying to figure out how "good" I was doing than I did looking for new ways to use it. It wasn't enough for me, even when my readings were growing stronger and becoming easier to see. For example, the physical location of the person whom I was reading became less and less of a factor. It was so different from case to case that I started to consider if connections and relationships were more important than distance between me and the subject of the vision, and the Panther just walked away shaking his head. Some unbidden visions have come to me from people within the same room, and others have come from across great distances. I wasn't actually looking at the person during any of these events. The red "slash" from their pain came to me as a clear vision with my eyes out of focus, as if the person's energy imbalance connected with my sensitivity field:

- a strained lower back while a person is working out miles away

- a person's neck pain at a restaurant

- a sore shoulder of a waiter in a bar

- a pulled lower back while a person was walking through a supermarket

- a pinched nerve in the center of the back from a person in a different country

- a pulled thigh muscle as a person enters a room

- a slap or buffeting of someone's leg while they were walking behind me, and I was facing the other direction

Even though I get these unexpected messages every now and then, I have made it my practice not to actively read people's energy if I am not invited to do so. I believe that there are respect and privacy codes for probing someone's energy, especially when it could result in a vision of their history that they don't wish to share. With that said, I'm sure it is a little disconcerting for the people I am eating with in a restaurant when I suddenly interrupt the conversation by gazing off into the distance and then whipping my head around, visually scanning the room. After looking around, I would locate someone several tables away with a red "slash" overlay of pain on him and then stare at him for a few moments.

Sometimes, I would look over there several times, until I identified the source of the physical discomfort in the person. So far, these spontaneous visions have all been about physical ailments. Will they go "deeper" into the emotional layer of people's energy as they pass by? I guess I will just have to find out, but I'm not sure I want it to develop into that.

My visions and their interpretations were only one source of confusion for me. My disbelief was extended when I started to actually feel some of the energy I perceived in my visions. During one Reiki session, I could see that my client was suffering from an upset stomach through the red "slash" of pain in her abdomen. As I examined her more closely, I began to perceive a thick, sticky clump of webbing strands connecting her Gut chakra and her Root chakra. The symbolism that came with these images informed me that she didn't trust her own decision-making process, and she second-guessed herself all the time. I moved to guide this tar-like webbing down her legs and out of her feet, but as I did so, I started to feel like my palms and fingers were stuck to this tar. I could feel the sensation of rolling clumps of tar off of my fingers, even though there was obviously nothing physically there on my hands. I have had my hands grow warmer during sessions, but this was one of the few times that my sense of touch interacted with the energy I was draining out of my subject. At that moment, I had an unusual vision. The woman was a little girl around six years old, running through some type of peaceful city park. She was in a nice little dress with nice shoes, and the accompanying messages informed me it was Easter. She was running from left to right in the vision, her arms outstretched toward someone. The vision panned over to the right to show me two adults, her parents, walking away from her to get into their car. Suddenly, they both stopped and spun around to face the little girl. The little girl folded her arms and started tapping one of her feet impatiently, her face covered in tears but her expression angry. I asked the woman, "Why am I seeing your parents leaving you behind in a park?" She didn't debate the vision I described to her; on the contrary, her face went flat with annoyance as she said, "They did that to me all the time..." I finished the Reiki session, continuing to drain those strands of negative energy out through her feet, until my hands felt like they were covered in slimy clumps of sticky goo. Rubbing my hands together did nothing to change the sensation. I finally opted to direct healing energy of my own into my hands to "scrape" this sludge from my hands, and my hands felt normal again. How could these tactile sensations be real? My intention was to pull this webbing out of her; it was so "sticky" that it left a residue of energy on my hands.

It may not seem immediately clear, but time is also a critical factor in Reiki healing. While I've never arrived at a complete answer as to why, I have learned that I have a certain affinity for the distance symbol. It is the most difficult symbol to draw, at least of the three to which I am attuned, but it was the first I wanted to learn. The distance healing symbol is also associated with the ability to move back and forth through time to apply healing. Time became very important to my Reiki readings after I started receiving visions of people's pasts, but the initial exploration of time healing was based on events my clients chose to discuss. For example, I had performed an initial reading on a woman with a lot of neck pain, and she was having headaches. She told me about her travel plans in a week to go visit her family for the Thanksgiving holiday, and that is when I saw the negative energy flowing from her Heart chakra to her Third Eye chakra. I told her that a lot of her current pain was due to the stress she was feeling about the pending visit; she was expecting a great deal of drama and unhappiness at seeing her family. Without really knowing how, I decided to mentally shift my perception *forward* in time to Thanksgiving and imagined myself as a bystander, viewing her walking into her parents' house. I sent some white healing light into that image to soothe the emotional angst, and then I shifted my perception back to the present. I questioned the Panther later about the power of healing people at different times in their lives, and he led me to my own answer by saying, "Well, which is harder to heal: physical pain or emotional pain?" People can often dwell on the emotional problems for months or even years, so it seems pretty logical (the Panther pronounced that word pretty sarcastically while making his point) that the founder of Reiki had discovered a way to treat the emotional wounds from a person's past as one of the causes of the person's issues in the present. The emotional pain we carry around with us affects us in so many ways.

A list of my arguments with the Panther over my Reiki abilities would not be complete without including the debates over whether or not the healing that I had imparted with my intention actually helped the recipient on some physical level. I found it easier to accept the visions I was receiving during the sessions than to accept the idea that I actually helped heal the problems I saw. (It sounds like the opposite should be true, but I never said my logic actually makes use of common sense when applied to Reiki.) I was having a conversation with a friend about the bizarre sensations that I had during the Reiki class I attended when he mentioned his interest in paranormal phenomena. He said that he might consider asking me to perform a Reiki reading on him, and suddenly, his energy aura was available to my sensitivity. I asked him if he wanted to know what I had just been shown, and he consented to a brief, impromptu reading. My sensitivity showed me that he was in pain as we spoke, the result of some type of muscle tear in his shoulder, behind his rotator cup. I could also see a red band of discomfort in his right knee. I tilted my head to the left, and I saw an overlapping image of a young man, obviously his son, connected to his Heart chakra. My friend was worried about his son's current direction in life, and it was adding to his emotional stress. He smirked and agreed that his son's recent activities have been challenging. Along with these issues, he told me that he had received some unfortunate news. Right at that moment, I saw a small cyst or mass in the lower part of his left lung. I probed the mass, and it appeared like a white lump, without the reddish indicators that showed some type of disease or infection. I asked his permission to work on him remotely, and I sent physical healing into him with the intent to reduce the size of that mass, breaking it apart piece by piece. I watched as my remote viewing showed the mass get smaller; the next x-rays he had done revealed the mass wasn't there. Did I actually help get rid of this cyst?

On another occasion, I decided to remotely work on another man who was recovering after cancer surgery in his throat. I didn't actually visit him in person, yet I seemed to be able to attune myself to his energy relatively easily. My sensitivity showed me the empty, carved-out space where many lymph nodes in his neck were removed. However, I looked more closely, and I saw unusual-looking tentacles radiating from his neck that contained small spheres of red disease. I interpreted these as cancerous nodules still in remaining his other lymph nodes. My Reiki healing traveled to the man to "knead" these masses and sear them with healing light to kill the cancerous cells. I worked on the man every night, and over time, I saw the nodules grow smaller, displaying less and less of the red hue that indicated the diseased cells. Finally, I could no longer see the masses in the lymph nodes. I'm happy to say that the next medical results showed that the man was cancer-free and recovering well from the surgery. Again, the doubt about my actual effectiveness in healing him came to mind. I finally asked the Panther if I had truly healed these men. His response was direct: "Does it really matter? You guided your healing intentions well, and they got better. You saw improvements while you were viewing them. Isn't that what's important?" He made a good point; the healing was the important outcome, regardless of my doubts on my contributions toward it.

My inner debates about my skills and effectiveness with Reiki didn't stop after these events, and they continue to this day. I still take nothing for granted, and I look for ways to explain everything I experience. But now, when something comes along that I can't explain, it strengthens my commitments and eagerness to practice energy healing, rather than distracting my focus and intention. When some vision or instinct comes along for which there is absolutely no way I could have made it up on my own, then the real fun begins.

Chapter 4: Medical Intuition

Let me tell you a little bit about my visions and how they occur. I haven't come up with another word for them, but I wish to avoid the possible connotations that they are necessarily religious or prophetic. My interpretation is that these messages are another expression of the energy that I read from the client. This amazing result of my Reiki study evolved over time. I consider the "chocolate heart" experience to be one of the first visions I had, but it was quite rudimentary compared to the future visions that came to me. The frequency of the visions was low when they first started, but as my sensitivity evolved, they started occurring with almost every Reiki session I performed. As I mentioned, from time to time I receive a brief vision outside of a session, just looking around a restaurant or passing by a person in a store, but these are limited to intuitive messages around someone's physical pain. I have experienced several different types of intuitive visions about my clients. When I "watch" one during a Reiki session, the client is almost always in the scene. I have had them while viewing a client with my eyes open and while my eyes are closed during the energy readings. The visions have come more often while my eyes have been shut, but I haven't felt the need to experiment with the frequency with each method; I accept the visions as they come.

The way a vision appears to me is a lot like watching a brief scene in a movie, a two-dimensional "video." When my eyes are open, it appears like a movie displayed by a computer projector connected to a laptop (or a 35mm reel-to-reel projector, for the less tech-savvy). Imagine a sheer screen of plastic about 8 or 9 inches in front of the client. With the projector pointing at the plastic sheet, the movie plays on the opaque sheet for three or four seconds, and then it stops. I can still see the person behind the screen on which it plays, but my "eyes" change their focus as I watch the scene flowing in front of them. When a vision appears to me while my eyes are closed, the color scene is isolated in the dark of my inner sight. It lasts a few moments and is gone. I find it interesting that I haven't forgotten any part of a vision I've received; the memories are clear and lasting, as if imprinted into my mind.

There is an additional component beyond the visual imagery that I receive during a Reiki vision. I was at a loss on how to define this component until recently. For me, it is the literal definition of extra-sensory perception (ESP). As the abridged movie plays, I receive mental insights and information, complimenting the scenes I am shown. Messages flood in about the scene, helping me to define the location, the emotional state of the "extras" in the movie, and even hints about the age of the client. There isn't a visual impression when these perceptions arrive; the thoughts manifest on their own, adding more details of both a physical and emotional nature, to help define the vision. As I describe my visions and readings, I would classify my Reiki and other energy reading abilities as mostly clairvoyant, being able to see physical problems, emotional challenges, and even events of the client's life. There is a bit of clairsentience involved, when I receive thoughts directly into my mind with information about the client. (It is at about this point when talking about ESP that my engineering mind starts acting like a petulant child: "La, la, la! I'm not listening to you!")

My Reiki examinations usually follow a pattern: physical identifications, emotional identifications, a vision of the past, and energy cleansing. I begin by identifying one or more physical ailments on the subject's body to address with the power symbol. After directing some initial healing to a few of these locations, I essentially "strip" that layer of energy away to read deeper or more subtle energies at the emotional level. In some ways, it is similar to having multiple sheets of plastic slides in a stack prepared from some presentation. The top few sheets have indicators of physical pain and problems drawn on them, and then I lift the top sheets up and out of the way to expose the lower sheets one at a time in order to take a look at the emotional and mental challenges. I move back and forth through these layers of energy to look for associations and links. Once I complete the initial readings and attune my energy to that of the client, I start wondering what insight I might receive in a vision connected to their lifeline or history. A vision doesn't necessarily have to relate to any of the issues I witnessed during my initial reading, so I simply accept the messages for what they are.

The content of a vision varies greatly, and they are complimented by message-laden images that provide insight into physical and emotional challenges the client has experienced. The physical challenges are often represented by a telltale bright-red swath or "slash" of color going across my field of vision, like a paintbrush stroke. I've developed a way to shift my perception from looking at the surface of a client to viewing his energy field, with a red "slash" of pain moving to a specific location on the body to help me locate a place to which I should guide healing energy. My visions concerning emotional challenges come in a variety of colors, usually related to the hue of the client's aura, yet they also include masses of dark or black negative energy with many different consistencies, like sticky webbing, chunky paste, or even thick oil.

Combining my studies with the visions I have experienced, I have built my definition of medical intuition to be the ability to use psychic or ESP powers to identify the root cause behind physical or emotional conditions. My Reiki sensitivity has grown stronger, even though my original belief was that the energy readings were limited to the client's current state of being. I was completely floored by the final vision type that I developed, and my evolution into a medical intuitive is a direct result of it: a vision of a past event within the client's life. Most people would agree that a person's history helps to shape him into the person that he is. If you are a proponent of the belief that time heals all wounds, I would argue that the statement needs to be expanded at the end with the phrase "if you LET it." Traumatic events tend to leave emotional scars upon people. Using Reiki to read the scars left by these events on the emotional state of a client is a first step toward helping to relieve the negative energy associated with them. The time component of emotional stress was one of the hardest concepts for me to wrap my head around, but the extra-sensory perceptions and the personal history I received during a Reiki vision came to me without a need to understand how things worked. When a vision showed me the client as a young adult or even as a child, I could sometimes even see the setting of the emotional event in the images, like a room of a house or an outdoor area. However, I could never explain how the supporting messages associated with the vision would inform me of the age of the person at that time. The visions I've had would not provide dates or years; the perceptions inform me how old the subject was at the time of the event as it unfolded. Is this how people evaluate time in their personal energy fields? Is this an interpretation of the messages I receive in a form that I could process for myself? I am still working on how to define these parameters of my readings, but there is no doubt that abuse and neglect experienced during a person's childhood leave a lasting impact on the emotional stability and physical health of the adult. Continuing the discussion on Reiki readings as a synchronization of my energy with emotional scars on the client's energy, I can see a possible explanation for the vision of a past trauma: a "recording" of the events and emotional turmoil upon a person's energy. I can then attune my sensitivity with this scar and tap into the stored imagery associated with it. In almost all of the visions I've had, I didn't have any prior knowledge of the painful events, so I am forced to conclude that the client's energy aura shows me these snapshots of the pain they experienced and have "carried around" with them.

A real turning point in my approach to Reiki took place a few months into my exploration of my skills, and I couldn't anticipate the far-reaching effects it would have on me. I was asked if I wouldn't mind hosting a Reiki session for a friend of a friend. I had never met the client before, but I was fine with the request. I was provided a little background information on the client concerning diagnoses of possible schizophrenia and family issues involved with a current relationship. My friend and I traveled to the client's home, and I asked the client to lie down on the couch. I began the Reiki session in my "normal" fashion, scanning for energy indications of physical conditions and problems. The initial Reiki scans showed me some blood flow issues in her legs, but I was surprised to see how readily the client's energy reacted to mine. I could "see" tingling in her hands, and her left foot became quite warm, both in my mind's eye and to the touch. With the feet being my chosen location to drain out negative energy from a client, the warming and energy flow to the feet seemed to be a good sign. I continued the examination, slowly probing more deeply into her energy flow. Another indicator I have developed in my lexicon of Reiki symbolism is related to the Crown chakra. My clients often show me some of their emotional states of self-pity, anger, or guilt by the resistance I detect while I am attempting to channel external healing energy in through the Crown chakra, and this client was no different. The clairsentient ESP images help to explain which and how many of these emotions are affecting the chakra closure, and I feel it is important that I make sure the Crown chakra is at least somewhat open before I end a session. Speaking in soft, soothing tones, I told her that she did deserve this healing, and that blaming herself for things outside of her control adds to the negative energy. I then worked to "pierce" some of the blockage in her Crown chakra. When I finally forced some of the white plasma of healing energy into the client, I received a vision I was completely unprepared for.

In a vivid vision, I suddenly saw an older child, with the overlaying ESP messages providing me an age of 12. The vision began as if I were seeing it through the child's eyes, looking downward. The vision drew me down to view the client's feet, wearing gray socks and standing on a floor with beige tiles. I was "informed" through intuitive messages that this was the client's family's kitchen, and then the vision panned upward to look around the room. She was facing a corner in the kitchen, and then the scene slowly spun around to face away from the corner. There was an island with a gray counter in the middle of the kitchen. The client focused on the counter, while a barrage of thoughts streamed in from the rest of the family to belittle and taunt her, and she was apparently being punished for some reason not disclosed in the scene. There were red and gray symbols of physical and emotional abuse with every family statement. I received the impression that instead of facing the corner, she was forced to face the family and watch them eat dinner while she went hungry.

I told the client about the scene after it was over, and her response was that this happened a lot. Her next comment was even more telling: "How did you know the color of my parents' kitchen floor?" The question boosted my confidence significantly, and I continued sharing what I had seen. I listened to how the family lamented the impacts these punishments had on her at the time. Right then, a stationary image appeared on her forehead, appearing as a black box on the right side of it. The image resembled a square manhole, and the cover was slightly ajar. The information that came to me showed that the client would take emotional refuge by opening this hatch and disassociating her primary persona from the abuse coming from the family. The client would "hide" her mental and emotional "cores" from the world and would assume a separate, dispassionate persona to resist the abuse. The client smiled and relaxed a little more, appreciating my interpretation that the "schizophrenic" personality shift could be controlled if she tried. After all, she had created it on her own to protect herself from her family's emotional torture.

The session continued, the images flowing to me as I worked to drain away the negative energy I found in her Solar Plexus chakra, indicating she didn't trust her own judgments. Within her apartment, her son was in the next room, taking a nap, and the son was the source from which the client drew her strength. A standalone image of the client as an angel with wings came to me, the wings wrapped around the child and a fierce look on her face. Right after this image faded, I received the message that the client was a survivor but was about to give up. I told the client about the angel vision, and I said that her mantra was the word "survive." The client was considering giving up, due to all of the struggles experienced in her life. I stated that in her despair, she had changed the word to "survived," as if the actions were over, yet the work and struggles would continue; the client needed to continue to focus on surviving. She might never been done with her struggles, but she had to look at them differently, as she had been so strong in the past through all of the childhood experiences I was shown. She could be strong for a little while longer.

The client's eyes popped open, and she stared at me with a mixture of wonder and disbelief. The client stood up, saying, "I don't know how you know what you do, but I really thank you for coming here today..." I was a bit confused, but the client turned around and lifted up her ponytail, unveiling a tattoo of an angel on the back of her neck, wings folded in front of it. After a moment, the client pulled the neck of her shirt lower, exposing her shoulders a little more. Across her shoulders, centered in the middle of her back, was a second tattoo of block letters spelling the word "SURVIVE."

My first reaction was to turn to my friend and say, "Oh...right...you must have told me about these tattoos before." As I turned, however, my friend was staring at me and was slowly shaking her head: "How could I tell you about those? I never knew about them myself..." I sat down on the couch, staring down at the square patterns of the carpet and trying to remember every detail of the vision and images that I saw. The client was a complete stranger; as of this writing, I have seen her only that one time in my entire life, yet my perceptions and messages during the Reiki session were amazingly accurate. This experience really challenged me; what rationale could I possibly come up with that would justify the idea that these thoughts came from my imagination? From a scientific viewpoint, this session could be seen as a "blind" experiment, with results that help support the validity of medical intuition. My imagination does have the potential to taint the results of the Reiki impressions, yet with *these* messages? On most occasions, I am trying to find a logical explanation to interpret the events that happen around me. With these experiences, I am hoping NOT to find one, in order to validate the clairvoyant nature of the experience. I've never found one, and the visions kept on coming.

On a few occasions, the visions I received actually showed me different scenes at multiple points across the person's past. Each time this happened, the initial visions were of the person as a child, and the subsequent scenes progressed through the person's life. I didn't receive them in a random sequence; they were shown to me in chronological order, as if I was supposed to see the evolution of the person's emotional state. One of these occasions was with a nervous woman who wasn't sure what the Reiki session would be like, and I saw three different snapshots of her childhood. The first vision was revealed within the initial ten minutes of my Reiki reading. It was one of the few visions in which there were intuitive messages that I had trouble interpreting. The initial scene was a young girl on roller skates. At the onset, I thought they were ice skates, but then I guided my visual perspective down to see the wheels on the skates. The extra-sensory information shared that she was seven years old, but I didn't feel the same clarity that was accustomed to when I mentally acknowledged this information. The little girl was skating around and fell, and the other little girls around her started laughing at her. I had also heard unseen male voices laughing. When I told the woman my interpretations, she told me that she was actually ten years old when she had her first pair of skates. I was still connected with the scene in the vision, and her confirmation of her age then expanded the images to show me a group of men on the other side of the makeshift skating rink, including her father. When the vision ended, I told her how I had seen a group of men pointing and laughing at her fall, and she simply said, "Those men were evil." I continued the Reiki readings and started to work on some of the negative energy I saw. (Her energy was very "demanding;" her leg kept twitching to "demand" that I get back to draining that gray, cement-like paste out of her feet faster.) The next vision I received let me know that this was the woman at age sixteen, sitting in her family's kitchen. Her parents were standing over her, berating her, yet the intuitive messages informed me that she hadn't done anything wrong to cause this yelling. She felt as nothing she did was good enough for them. She agreed that this kind of thing happened often at that point in her life, and I quickly received the third vision of the Reiki session during her acknowledgement. The messages associated with the scene notified me that she was nineteen at this point, and she was becoming more and more rebellious against her parents. Fleeting images showed me that she was staying out all night and getting more involved with boys, none of which she hid from her parents. I smiled slyly when I told her that she was getting to be a "naughty girl," and she told me, "When I was nineteen, I moved out of the house." I finished the session by drawing out some of the negativity and relaxing her. She claimed that she felt the energy connections strongly and thanked me for my work. With everything that is done to children by their parents, their family, or even strangers, it's rewarding to be able to show the adult that there is some type of relief from these burdens.

Even through all of this, I still held reservations for many months about how I could classify my Reiki skills in my own mind. Throughout my life, I have practiced carefully choosing my words in an attempt to reflect my impressions, feelings, and opinions as specifically as I could. I am well aware of this practice in my conversations with others, and I try to listen to my own word choices to give me more insight on both conscious and subconscious impressions I have. This applies to both what I say and do not say. Throughout all of the received perceptions, visions, and client feedback of my Reiki sessions, both in-person and remotely, I called Reiki a "power" that I had learned. To me, my selection of that word means I was still coming to terms with accepting it. I feel it is important to share the experience that made me let down my resistance, changing my description from a "power" to call it a "gift." The experience that led to this transformation of my feelings took place due to a friendly challenge; who knew you could learn so much about Reiki in the lobby of a motel, with your mother standing right next to you?! (I also want to give my mother credit for naming me a medical intuitive long before I could accept my own definition of my Reiki skills. This helped me categorize myself. As you will see in a later chapter, I was forced to re-evaluate this gift of energy sensitivity once again. I guess I should expect this to happen in the future as things continue to evolve...)

My mother and I were checking out of the motel, and we had become friends with the manager, a truly gracious person and very in tune with herself. Walking into the lobby on the morning of our departure, my mother was the one to broach the subject of Reiki, beginning to discuss what she observed in a session I held the night before, but I immediately asked her not to share the stories, and she accepted my wishes without question. My choice of making my stories about my clients as generic as possible is part of the respect I want to maintain for the people who have asked me for their help; some things should remain anonymous, leaving it up to the individual to reveal them. My mother was given permission to sit through the session, and she understood the personal nature of the revealed visions. My unexpected client, the manager, also accepted my request, but then she surprised me by asking me to "read" her. She laughed when she said that I was being put on the spot. She stepped out from behind the counter so that I could see her entire body, and she folded her arms. I chuckled and informed her that "it doesn't really work that way." I wasn't originally planning to try a reading at all, but then something tugged at my mind, at the edge of my sensitivity. I tilted my head a little to the right, and I looked her up and down for about three seconds, attuning myself to her energy. Suddenly, a flood of visions came to my mind's eye, along with a series of perceptions about each vision. (Maybe it DID work that way, after all...)

In rapid succession over the span of only 15 seconds, I relayed what I saw almost as quickly as I received the images:

- A pinkish hue on her feet, with swelling in the feet and lower legs, and a view of energy being clogged before it could flow down past her ankles: "Well, I can say that I see you have a circulation problem with your feet; something has recently cut off some of the blood to them..."

- An unusual band of reddish pain starting at the top of the back of the neck, going down and splitting into two branches, leading into each shoulder blade: "And I also see that you have a problem with the base of your neck, affecting both of your shoulders, like some kind of slipped disc or pinched nerve. It looks like an upside-down goal post in [United States] football..."

- A strange image of her Gut chakra transforming into a closed box, and then the box splitting into two different boxes, along with ESP thoughts explaining the symbolism: "Oh, now I see you have an important decision to make, and you are afraid of making the wrong one..."

- And while I was describing the two boxes, a narrow black filament of negative energy appeared from the Gut chakra and led up to the Throat chakra, filled with dark gray ooze associated with silence: "And I see that you haven't told anyone about this decision, not even your family..."

Her arms slowly unfolded as she stood in silence, and she blinked a few times as her mouth fell open. She looked at my mother, and my mother folded her arms and simply said, "Well, you ASKED him..." My challenger proceeded to describe her thoughts on what I had "seen." She told me she had started running on a treadmill, and her feet were hurting. She did confirm that she had back pain that led up into her neck as well. It took her a moment to collect herself and say "yes" to the decision vision, and she said she hadn't told anyone about it. (To this day, I don't know what this decision was or if it has ever been resolved. I will add, however, that I had an intuitive message that suggested what it might be. Since she didn't share it, I didn't pry. I may ask her at some point in the future...) I was already amazed at myself and how quickly the images came to me and how extensively the associated extra-sensory messages provided details, but the readings didn't stop there.

My challenger then started to describe a meeting she attended, looking to share something that took place at some conference. As I stood there listening, a vision just above her right shoulder began to manifest. It resembled a solid, lumpy gray mass, like thick spackle, and without warning, the clump slid off of her shoulder and fell away, disappearing before it hit the floor. I immediately interrupted the story about the meeting and interjected the messages I received about this mass:

"At this meeting, something happened to you that you weren't prepared for. Always before, you were very strict in your religious beliefs. If you could not find it in the scriptures, then you would not accept it as truth. Whatever happened at this conference surprised you enough that you weren't ready for it. You couldn't raise your rigid 'wall of defense' to resist the message, so you looked at it in a different light. Something happened, and it was like this great weight slid off of your shoulder without you realizing it until later. Now, instead of defining your truth by scripture, you use your own beliefs and defend them by finding references to them in scripture. It sounds like a subtle difference, but it changed you significantly..."

By now, the person was nodding, almost unconsciously. She described an event at a meeting in which the leader made a rather out-of-place statement that took her off guard, and her friend who was sitting next to her slumped out of her chair. "The lecturer actually said that some of you may feel like there is a weight sliding off of your shoulder," she added, staring at me with a slowly growing smile.

After a few moments, she described another event in which she went to a store and found the owner lying in a bed in the back room. The owner of the store was stricken with cancer. When she found this out, she asked if it would be ok to pray for the owner. After a brief prayer, she touched the knee of the older man, and she felt the man's leg pulse. Several weeks later, she went back to the store, and she was informed that the owner was now diagnosed as cancer-free. During the story, my perception shifted to view the prayer scene as if I was in the store. I saw her touch the afflicted man, and I watched a shockwave of energy run up the owner's leg and into his Heart chakra. I explained my interpretation of the event as her sharing of some healing energy with the old man but also "reminding" the man that cancer was not always the definition of his life. He was once healthy and active, and his despair and negative emotional energy had also clouded his self-image, so that he had forgotten that he did have some ability to heal himself. Despair is so debilitating, but coming out of despair can be so energizing; Reiki taught me that.

Speechless, my challenger slowly extended her hand to shake mine. After she held my hand for a moment, she pulled me into a hug, showing her appreciation for the sharing of my insights and visions. My mother and I left the hotel lobby and walked to our car quietly, until my mother finally broke the silence, "I think you just found a believer in your gifts..." My response: "Yeah...me."

Each time we have visited Tombstone, we have tried to make time to see our new friend. On another occasion, we stopped by just to say hello, and she had just arrived at the building. After asking about how our trip was going, she mentioned that she was in a good deal of pain...and then she paused, smiled, and looked up at me, saying, "Well?" I knew she was asking me if I could see anything with my sensitivity, and I was already noting this red "slash" of pain on her left shoulder at the base of her neck. The painful energy flow traveled up past her jaw to her left temple. I told her that she had a lot of stress, associated with some emotional energy, on her left shoulder. She said that it was still amazing to her that I could tell on which side she was in pain. As she was talking, I had a brief vision of her gritting her teeth in frustration and holding in a good deal of tension. I interrupted her and said, "Do me a favor. Humor me, and try something? Take a deep breath in through your nose, and release it slowly out of your mouth. Let your jaw relax; let your mouth hang open naturally. When you exhale, focus on that knot in your left shoulder, and imagine that you could let the tension calmly flow out of your mouth when you exhale out." To the credit of the relationship we have built, she immediately stopped her story and started the deep-breathing exercise. I watched her as a smile slowly spread across her face: "How did you DO that?" I responded, "I didn't; you did. I just saw how you were holding a lot of tension inside of you, and a lot of it was collecting in your shoulder. Keep doing that little exercise today, and help yourself feel a little better."

My continuing practice of my Reiki skills seems to have made it "easier" for me to attune my reading to an individual in the future after I have already successfully connected to the person's energy once before. My explanation of this is that my Reiki healing ability syncs up with the person's energy field to interact and analyze the ebb and flow of the critical chakras. Once I have identified the person's energy, it is easier for me to adapt my energy in the future to match his the next time I try. My scientific mind accepts this more readily than many things that happen to me with Reiki. This is like one energy field being altered to match the frequency and amplitude of another field. When they merge, the first field becomes amplified, making it easier to "see" its properties. When I can see it more easily, I can attune to it more quickly.

One friend was interested in hearing about my Reiki experiences after seeing how excited I was with one of my sessions that resulted in an incredible vision. She approached my desk, put out her hand so that I might grasp it, and said, "Can you read me?" I hadn't described my full Reiki process yet, so I told her that I actually preferred not to make any physical contact with someone during my initial assessment period. However, I thought that maybe I should do a little experiment, so I did take her hand in mine. As I expected, I didn't feel any energy flowing through the contact, but it also didn't impede my Reiki sensitivity, either. I performed a quick reading over her energy while standing in front of her. I quickly saw that she had a telltale red "slash" in the middle of her right shoulder blade, and I received a brief ESP message that this was from some type of exercise she had done. When I told her this, she stared at me for a moment and said, "Not even my kids know about that; the only person I told was my husband." While she was making this statement, I looked down at her knee to see another red band of pain in her knee, but this one had a thin red line leading down to her foot. I told her that she had also hurt her foot, and she was changing her gait, now causing problems in her knee. Her response as she laughed was, "Ok...this is getting creepy..." A few weeks later, both of us were walking down the same hallway in opposite directions. As she recognized me and waved, I was shown a vision of her bending forward and shoveling snow, straining her back. The red splash of color going down from her shoulder to her lower back lingered for a few moments after the vision disappeared. All I said to her was, "You gotta let that husband of yours shovel the snow." She laughed and almost unconsciously raised her hand to her back, saying, "I know, right?! I feel like I just...hey! Did you just SEE my back pain?" I just smiled knowingly and kept walking past her.

There have been Reiki sessions in which I was invited to perform a reading, but I had to overcome the person's "defenses" before I could attune myself to his energy. During one reading, my client had the ability to encase herself in a shimmering neon-green shield, not unlike the one I generate around myself in white, and I immediately wondered if she was a sensitive. I was unskilled at trying to pierce someone else's shield - I had never had to even attempt it before - and I was a bit confused as to why I was being shut out even after being invited to perform the reading. I asked the Panther to come help me find a way to get through this green defensive shell. He appeared next to the client and began to pace back and forth, until he finally looked at me and drew my eyes down to a tiny pinhole in the area of her Heart chakra, and then I knew exactly what to do. I saw an emotional link that I followed through the green shield, and I was finally able to read her energy. Perhaps some of the visions I received were part of the reason for the shielding. The first vision was her as a child, around age 7, and she was a happy, active little girl, completely in love with her grandfather. While I didn't see the details, I received intuitive messages that her grandfather had passed away at that time, and I could see the toll it took on her, changing her personality over the next two or three years. Later in the session, I viewed a much more symbolic vision than I was used to; normally, I will see actual excerpts of a person's life, but this vision was much more abstract. I was shown that around age 21, she had an important relationship with an unknown man end in pain, and it hurt her deeply. I could see my client on the left side of the vision, but the man standing next to her on the right of the vision was just a dark silhouette. The silhouette tore away from my client's image and began to crumble into dust. My client confirmed that she was in a bad relationship at that time, and I suddenly saw a continuation of the previous vision. The silhouette stopped crumbling and changed from gray to black. The silhouette was suddenly thrown to the right, falling into a boiling, steamy pit of magma that hadn't been in the previous vision. I opened my eyes, looked at my client, and said, "...and you got even with him, didn't you?" She smiled at me and said, "Damn right, I did..." I can see how this pain, carried forward through many years, can make someone want to hide from an emotional reading. I also developed a new-found respect for the words, "Hell hath no fury like a woman scorned."

Sometimes, the shielding around a client is due to nervousness and worry about what I might see. A different client once asked me to read her, but she was having a hard time becoming relaxed. She squirmed and laughed nervously while I was trying to begin my initial reading, continuing to apologize for her behavior. I didn't tell her at the time that I had already performed my initial assessment; I wanted to see how it would change as we proceeded. Covering her body from head to toe, there was a silky "veil" acting like a thin shield attempting to block my reading. I had already pierced this veil, making a large hole just above her Gut chakra, so I was able to see the nervousness that generated it. I was then shown a thin line leading from this veil into her Heart chakra, and I realized she didn't want me to attune to her feelings of resentment. She felt guilty about them, but they were there nonetheless. When I revisited her Gut chakra, I could see what appeared to be a cylindrical "hole" in her gut, and it was filled with charcoal-like gravel, reminding me of a coffee can full of wet grounds. The intuitive messages with this vision told me she didn't trust her own feelings. She felt like her family demanded so much of her that she has no time to pursue anything for herself. I was able to help some of that negative gravel flow up out of the hole and down her legs, drawing the negativity out of her feet.

Finally, there was one Reiki session in which I had no way to directly confirm the visions and intuitions I was receiving. However, it was a particularly rewarding experience for me to be working on this client. Due to an unfortunate incident, the daughter of a good friend of mine has some significant challenges with communication, both mental and physical, due to a terrible anaphylactic reaction that affected many of her body's systems. Honestly, I was a bit ashamed when I realized that I had not thought about going to visit my friend sooner to perform a Reiki session on her daughter, but I have come to grips with the notion that I still don't "actively" think of myself as a Reiki healer, sometimes overlooking it completely (in much the same way I overlook Reiki when I could be using it to heal myself, as you will see in the next chapter). I traveled to my friend's house, not really knowing what to expect, and she showed me to her daughter's room. I could sense that my friend was a little tense. She was going to leave me alone in the room with her daughter, but I let her know that it was perfectly fine if she wanted to stay and watch. She sat down for part of the session as I walked around her daughter's bed. At first, I wasn't really sensing anything from the girl when I started my energy reading. I couldn't tell if I was expecting too much or if I couldn't read her energy for one reason or another. Finally, I asked the Panther to help me find her energy points on which I should focus, since she couldn't tell me herself. In an amazingly gentle gesture, the Panther climbed up on the wide hospital bed and lay down horizontally at the head of the bed, with the girl's head resting gently against his furry side. As adorable as this may sound, the funny image of an 800-pound cat trying to find a way to balance its huge body at the head of a bed without having its legs and head slide off the edge and crash to the floor kind of ruins the mood, yet the Panther did an admirable job with this risky maneuver. What surprised me was not his success at climbing up onto the bed but the intuitive message I received about how the girl had actually felt his presence there. I could see their energies connect, and I told my friend about the energy exchange that I had just seen between the Panther and her daughter.

Now that I had synced up with her energy, I was able to begin reading her emotional energy layer. I was sad to see that she felt a certain level of guilt about her current circumstances, and I wasn't about to ignore that feeling; she had no reason, whatsoever, to feel guilty. I gave her my emotion crystal to hold, and she gripped it tightly. As I started talking to her during the session, her mother walked out of the room to get something. Just then, I was shown an interesting vision of a proud day in the girl's life at age 8; she was at a go-cart race track, driving a car by herself and beating everyone in her family to the finish line. The vision told me the general direction of this track from the family's home, and when I pointed off to my left when my friend came back into the room, she confirmed that there was a race course not too far away in that direction. At that point, I took the crystal from the girl's hands and asked my friend to hold onto it and focus on it. My friend couldn't believe how warm the crystal was, and I asked her to keep holding it for a while. The race track finish line wasn't the only vision I received; later in the session, I was shown the little girl as she looked on the present day, in the clothes she was wearing. She was looking at me while making a strange gesture: her left arm was stretched out to the side, and her right arm was bent in front of her chest, moving up and down. I couldn't figure out the significance of the action, and there weren't any additional messages accompanying it, but I made a note of it.

After the session, I talked to my friend about what I had seen and how impressed I was that her daughter had been able to connect with both the Panther and me. Her older daughter came home and joined in on the conversation when I was talking about the race track and how her little sister was showing me how proud she was about beating her older sister in that race. The older sister then made a comment on how the younger one was always winning when they played those video games that simulate playing a guitar; apparently the little girl beat everyone in the house, including her father, who was an actual guitar player. Hold on - THAT is what she was showing me?! That odd gesture of moving her hand up and down was *strumming a guitar*?! I was convinced that, in spite of her current challenges, I had successfully communicated with her on an energy level she was able to understand, and that was a very promising sign. All in all, it was an amazing session, and I will certainly be going back soon to continue my work with this lovely young lady.

Overall, the ease with which I started receiving these visions and the barrage of extra-sensory messages that comes with them still surprises me at times. It seems pretty logical that I would want to learn more about medical intuition when I am receiving intuitive thoughts with the clairvoyant images of a person's pain. These rapid-fire images provide insights and sometimes explanations for how to interpret what I am seeing in the visions, allowing me to build a frame of reference. When I consider how I can walk into a restaurant and receive images of another patron's physical distress, I become even more motivated to learn what I can about the extent of this gift. Seeing other people's pain lets me figure out how to focus my energy and intention to invoke healing for them. I just wish I could figure out how to get better at healing myself.

Chapter 5: Self-Healing

The topic of self-healing has come up in my mind at many different points during my evaluation of this new awareness. Even now, I struggle with the concept to the continuing frustration - and secret enjoyment - of the Panther. I'm sure he questions just how "aware" I really am if I can't even figure out how to heal myself, but he continues to support my efforts with a certain amused patience. During our shared meditation periods, there seems to be no end to his enjoyment at poking fun at what he calls my "avoidance logic" when I think about how to heal myself. As usual, there is little point in arguing with the Panther; he is usually right, and he can just disappear when debate starts to go against him. (It has happened a few times, but I think he leaves because he wants me to deal with the situation myself, just so I ultimately realize that he was right to begin with...)

Remember, this whole journey into exploring Reiki started with an unexpected side effect of a self-massage. For most of my life, I have had a problem on the left side of my neck and my left shoulder. That muscle group is susceptible to a lot of tension, knotting up on many occasions. There have been many times at which I was coming down with a cold or developing a flu, and the hard knotting of my muscles in my neck caused severe headaches that signaled the oncoming illness. I can also have muscle-tension headaches in that cord of muscles due to sleeping with my neck at a bad angle. With this spot being a constant source of pain and discomfort, I have developed some skill at massaging out the knots and applying pressure at specific points to improve the blood flow through the muscle cords. In effect, I have been performing some minimal amount of self-healing for a long time with this condition. One day a few months before my Reiki training class, I was massaging the tension in my neck without paying much attention to what I was doing. After a few moments, I noticed that the skin on my neck started to ache, like a slight chafing or abrasion. When I focused my attention on the area, I felt how warm the skin was. The heat was comforting, but it wasn't until later that I realized the heat came from the palm of my hand. I was surprised that I could still feel the heat radiating from my palm even without actually touching my neck. I started experimenting with mentally focusing on channeling heat out of my hands to warm my neck, and it became something I could do upon command. It is a useful tool on a cold winter night when I want to heat up the blankets of my bed, too. This does consume some of my own personal energy, yet it has evolved into the ability to raise my body's overall heat generation whenever I desire. The heated muscle-tension massages are more effective for the pain than the ones without, yet they also had an unexpected "side effect," becoming the source of my interest in Reiki. When I told a friend about this new ability, I found out that this kind of laying of hands was one of the standard procedures of Reiki healing. I admit that I wasn't all that interested in the Reiki class, but I hoped it would help me find new and better ways to use this heat channeling ability. Of course, the presence of an 800-pound panther leaning on your thigh during the first exercise of a Reiki practitioner training session can divert your attention from what you originally wanted.

It's reassuring that I do feel a certain level of relief after a session of working on my own physical ailments. It turns out that, sometimes, I can possibly, maybe, on occasion, overthink things just a bit when I am trying to classify them. (There are people out there right now saying, "Tell me something I DON'T know...") When it has been successful, my self-healing is quite rewarding; it's my practice of performing a self-evaluation of the blockages or pain that often leads to my overlooking the obvious. In my eagerness to disassociate my mind and imagination from the evaluation to make it "pure," I have spent extensive amounts of time focusing on creating an unbiased evaluation and not enough on using common sense. In spite of how the Panther disarms me with his own logic, he hasn't been able to convince me to stop focusing so much on the self-evaluation process, as it makes me lose sight of the overall goal: to actually heal the issues. As a Reiki practitioner, the healer receives the added benefit of crystal attunement; once the Reiki healer has become attuned to his personal crystals, he can then share in the healing energy that he is channeling into a client. I learned that it's a bit different when I set out to heal myself. I always thought that having a "free" energy healer at my disposal 24 hours a day would be a great thing, but it turns out I don't do a very good job of it when I am my own client.

I am a bit embarrassed to admit that it took me at least four months of practicing Reiki on OTHER people before it occurred to me that maybe I should actually try healing myself when I wasn't feeling well. I had strained my knee, something that I do every now and then due to a damaged ACL, and the swelling and pain were increasing. In one of those "HEYYY!" moments that made me feel pretty foolish afterward, I finally "remembered" that I was a certified Reiki practitioner, so I started the preparations, clearing my chakras and cleansing my energy to initiate a self-reading for identifying my physical and emotional states. Unfortunately, I didn't feel like my initial readings were going well; I couldn't see any specific emotional or physical issues in my readings, and the pain in my knee was distracting. My solicitous Panther was so helpful:

Panther: "I'm here if you need me…"

Me: "I can't figure this out; maybe I am trying too hard…"

Panther: "Oh? What are you trying to do?"

Me: "I am trying to read myself for the reasons for my pain."

Panther: (blinking twice with a flat expression) "Are you kidding me??"

Me: "It's frustrating. I can't seem to attune my mind to my current state."

Panther: (looking down at the ground and shaking his head) "Wow...I am speechless."

Me: "Well, can you guide me toward the problem?"

Panther: "What are you TALKING about?! Why the heck are you trying to "read yourself" to identify the source of your own physical pain?! You already KNOW the problem! Just work on healing it!"

Me: "Yeah, but I want to see if there are other things going on. That's what I normally do for the first 20 minutes of a Reiki session."

Panther: "How about you just focus on the knee, since you already know the problem, and save that mental health check for when I am NOT around?! If you REALLY feel the need to go through that self-exam, do me a favor: wait till I'm gone! Hey, look at that! I just saved you 20 minutes! You're welcome!"

Me: (sheepishly) "Umm, thanks..."

Panther: (rolls his eyes) "Nice logic on THAT one..." (departs)

In hindsight, it was a great learning experience to show me that you cannot really see past your own choices. It's almost as important to know *why* you make a choice as it is to actually make it. I kept dealing with my own healing the same way I treated other people's issues, at times following procedure for procedure's sake when it wasn't needed. Of course, this doesn't mean that my next few attempts at self-healing went that much more smoothly; how did I miss learning from my mistakes when they were pointed out so...directly? At least I spent less time trying to perform those initial scans on myself. The next self-healing attempts were focused solely on physical discomfort. Muscle pulls, headaches, and sprains were minor injuries, and it was easier to drive my Reiki intention inward when I could feel the discomfort. Pulling energy from the healing plane and channeling it into myself took a little practice, but I learned to guide it through my own Crown chakra to the affected areas.

With Reiki, as with many other things, you can sometimes face the notion that "you don't know what you don't know." This can be particularly meaningful in the middle of a surprising experience during a self-healing session. Ailments or issues can be revealed during the simplest exercises, and you may not even know what you are looking at until you analyze it. One example of a standard exercise is cleansing your personal energy before a reading in order to help attune yourself to the client's energy. The exercise includes shielding and grounding yourself and then looking to strip away any negative energy you may find. On this occasion, I was going through the exercise that I was now pretty familiar with when I felt a "snag" during the cleansing. Forming the shield was fine. I had no problem with grounding my energy, either. When I got to the point of siphoning my energy through my own mental sieve, something unknown got stuck on the mesh. At first, I noticed only the sensation of being stuck, like the feeling of having the strap of a bag hanging on your shoulder get caught on a door handle; you walk through the door, but then you are yanked backward. I wasn't really paying attention while going through the filtering procedure, so it was kind of surprising to feel like something was hooked on the metaphysical sieve. I mentally tugged on my energy that had already passed through the sieve, and only then did I realize that there was some actual blockage preventing me from directing the rest of my energy through it.

When I looked down at my torso, I saw this strange circular loop, not unlike a fishing hook, sticking out of my Solar Plexus chakra. I was a bit startled, so I probed the hook without removing it, and it seemed to consistently change colors from black to red and back. In this vision, I grasped the hook and received intuitive symbolism indicating that it was an emotional bond that someone had affixed to me, and I wasn't consciously aware of it. The sensations I received during that brief mental "contact" revealed that this hook was some undesirable tie to my energy that I had unwittingly allowed. In the same way as you would remove a hook from a fish you have caught, I slowly rotated the hook to guide it out of my energy. When I got to the barbed tip, I gingerly fed it through the leftover "hole" in my energy field, and I could feel the twinge when I finally pulled it out. This was all new to me, so I decided to send healing to the small tear where the hook had pierced my energy in order to help close it. Before I mentally tossed this hook away, I used my own energy to sever this end of the cord to avoid another attempt at attachment. Finally, I was able to proceed with my energy cleansing and get to work on the client. This experience helped me recognize that there are many things to seek out during a self-analysis; the things you don't know sometimes can "hurt" you.

Depending upon the scope of an injury and the intensity of the pain I am going through, self-healing never even occurs to me as an option. A real test of my commitment to Reiki self-healing arose when I passed kidney stones. The overwhelming pain and nausea from what felt like pushing a jagged piece of quartz through a coffee stirrer in my lower back banished even the thought of the basic Reiki symbols from my mind. Writhing around in agony isn't very conducive to meditation and focus. I went through at least five bouts of nauseating pain as the stone continued to move; there was no way I was going to be able to focus my extra-sensory perceptions on my kidney tube in the middle of this blazing torture. When the stone finally traveled its course, I was left utterly drained, but I managed to draw in white healing energy to help the internal wounds and let me heal some of the damage. I had no energy of my own to spare for this process. At that point, I didn't care that my Reiki ability is more effective when I weave my own energy into the healing. I went through the energy summoning procedures in a very detached way.

Lucky me, I was given a second chance to prove my Reiki sensitivity to myself, but did it really have to be through passing *another* kidney stone?? The agony of the second stone took place less than a week later, and I chose pain killers over self-guided intention and healing. Checking myself into a local emergency room, the nurses started a medicated intravenous treatment. For hours, I rolled back and forth on the hospital bed, not really feeling any kind of relief. When I calmed my mind in between early-morning reruns from the 1990s on the TV in my room, I closed my eyes, and immediately, there was a welcome flash of emerald-green feline eyes. A slight smile, the first in 24 hours, crossed my face, and I guided myself deeper into meditation. I was able to lean on one side, and I directed universal white healing energy into my back from the outside. At the same time, I added my own energy to the healing by channeling heat out of my hand while massaging the traumatized area. Within moments, the pain subsided, and the muscle spasms were quieted. Once again, my scientific mind wasn't ready to accept that it was my healing skill, and not the onset of the medication's effects, that was helping my back and kidneys, so I stopped the Reiki massage. Five minutes later, the agony returned, and the spasms were worse than ever. I ground my teeth for about 20 minutes in response to the waves of pain, trying to prove something to myself that could not possibly have been as important as giving myself relief. Finally, I resumed the Reiki massage, and I drove away the convulsing pains. In the next hour, the nurse returned and asked me how I was feeling. I didn't really want to face a possible debate about the principles and benefits of Reiki in a hospital emergency room, but I said, "Well, I don't know what you are dripping into me, but it isn't working at all. I am doing better, though; my own Reiki massage is taking care of the pain." The nurse responded, "Really? Hmm...do you want to Reiki-massage me?" No, that's ok; I just wanted out of that place. It didn't occur to me until later that the emergency room nurse didn't ask what Reiki was and didn't challenge me on its effectiveness over the drugs. Her reaction didn't really change anything in my mind one way or the other, but I did take note that she seemed to at least accept the situation from my perspective.

I do need to spend some time describing how detrimental the consequences of "forgetting" the benefits of Reiki self-healing can really be. Walking around with sore knees, a twinging back, or a throbbing headache seems a bit foolish if you can do something about it through Reiki. But suffering through physical distress pales in comparison to what I went through during the emotional turmoil of a depression. I have already described how emotional pain can leave "scars" on a person's energy aura. Oh how I wished I had tried Reiki sooner! Emotional depression usually alters a person's mental state, even if the person's own mind created the feelings of hopelessness that put him out of reach of any help. With my eternal optimism and my confidence in myself, I found it very hard to predict the possibility of my sinking into a depression. Feelings of hopelessness and a desire to simply hide from myself added to the downward spiral, and I was ill-prepared to deal with it. I didn't recognize the signs until it was far too late. The associated loss of appetite just led to less physical energy, so I couldn't expend much on my own behalf, even if it had actually crossed my mind to try. The constant reliving of the perceived problems effectively gave me insomnia, and we all know what a chronic lack of sleep can do to our physical state and our mental disposition.

Afterward, I felt a little foolish when I didn't use my own Reiki gift to treat some of the despair, but it was the furthest thing from my thoughts while stewing in my own lethargy. The sleepless nights were horrible; hoping to function during the day after waking up every 30-40 minutes throughout the night was futile. A full day of numbing hopelessness just made it worse, piling on the negative emotional energy and blinding me to how I might break the circle of paralysis. On the third night of minimal sleep, I became delirious, complaining to myself how badly I needed sleep. Thank goodness some subconscious insight breached the gray fog of my indifference and numbness, and at 4:18 am, I shifted my perception and decided to complain to the Panther instead: "Can't YOU help me sleep?!"

A vision came unbidden to me in the dark of the morning. The Panther came to help me, but he had to leap across a huge chasm to reach me. He crouched down, his muscles taut, and he leapt into the air, soaring preternaturally fast over a gulf of shadow that was radiating from me. He landed with a thud that I actually felt rippling through me, making the "ground" shake in this vision. He came over and pressed his sleek, soft forehead against mine and then filled me with soothing energy: "Don't you know that you have to ASK for my help?!"

This is one of the very few times that I was frustrated with the Panther, rather than vice versa, but it wasn't really his fault. I was already aware that Spirit Guides usually respect our individuality and don't intrude unless invited. Now that I had summoned him, the Panther immediately showed me a large representation of the emotional healing symbol right in front of my eyes. I built a mental connection from my Third Eye chakra to the symbol, making the connection as large as I could. Wordlessly, he guided me through how to funnel the oppressive negative energy out of my Third Eye and into the symbol, and I could actually feel my spirit becoming lighter. After at least two full minutes of expelling the black viscous fluid representing the depression, I was so drained that I fell asleep immediately, and I slept for five hours. When I awoke, I was ready to face myself and pull my emotions out of the pit of despair I had built for myself. I started talking to the Panther about my state of mind that led up to the depression, and I continued draining my heavy feelings into the giant emotion symbol that I summoned. I finally integrated myself back into the world around me, promising to remember the wisdom and the "fine print" of the Panther's guidance: asking for help leads to finding help...and my appetite came back immediately; I was RAVENOUS! That might have been one of the best peanut butter sandwiches I have ever had!

In times of my own need, it took a conscious effort to control and guide my intention and energy. At other times, the healing I have received from Reiki and the Panther came in the forms of reinforcement and revelation. In many ways, the attraction I continue to feel when delving into the exploration of healing and paranormal energy lies in the unknown, the unexpected rewards that range from a small twinge of satisfaction to a massive unveiling of truth. The lessons learned aren't always ones that I anticipated or actively sought.

Oddly, I had an assumption when I first started practicing distance healing that the required concentration and focus would not be possible while driving a car. I am happy to be wrong about this. During long commutes, for example, investing the time in distance healing sharpens my spiritual perceptions and sends positive intention and energy out to friends and family in need. It also helps to reduce the road rage I develop after dealing with all of the "other" idiots on the road. (Note I chose the word "reduce" and not "remove" for my road rage; I still have some work to do on that front...) However, this particular instance of revelation was the only time the Panther has ever specifically asked me to heal someone. I am a little ashamed that I resisted his request for as long as I did. In my defense, there are reasons that help explain my reluctance. The Panther wasn't interested in any of them. He won this dispute, as usual. Illuminated over the span of about thirty minutes, the truths of spiritual power and selfless healing that I learned will never be forgotten. On the other hand, talking out loud to a feline Spirit Guide while doing 70 mph down a highway does make one think twice about one's mental stability. At least I could deal with my "insanity" by myself, without having someone ask, "Ummm, who are you talking to?"

While merging onto a highway, a vision of the Panther's large face appeared in front of me. After waiting a moment to confirm that he had my attention, his face slid to the right, and a person's face appeared in my vision from the left to replace his. By this point in my Reiki experience, I knew what these visual symbols meant: I was supposed to send remote healing to this person. I wasn't going to accept THIS task without a fight. This person would NEVER have accepted my support, let alone my healing. This person wanted nothing to do with me at all, and I could not think of a single scenario in which my "interference" would have been tolerated. I began to argue the Panther's unspoken request out loud in the car.

"Ohhh, no...no...NO...no, no, no, no...not him, no..."

The Panther's face appeared in front of me again, with a calm but unblinking gaze directly into my eyes. Then he summoned the person's face again. Still in denial, I tried a different tact: using the tenets of Reiki itself.

"No...not this time...this person would never welcome my energy. Besides, it would be wrong to reach out and intrude upon another person's energy without permission. I am supposed to be invited to help, and I don't...think..."

My words faded away as the scene changed. For the first and only time since we started this journey together, the Panther was furious with me, and I could feel it as well as see it. When he returned a third time, he came at me in full force, his entire body in the vision taking up the span of the windshield. He was crouched down, muscles taut, teeth bared, ears pinned back. His huge claws tore at the air in front of me. He sent wave after wave of psychic energy crashing into my personal shield. I wasn't afraid; that was not his intent. I was humbled and sat in awe of him. This was a power far beyond my own, and he was showing me just what he could do...

Through gritted teeth, he discarded his normal sarcasm and spoke bluntly: "You WILL do this. Your excuses are irrelevant, so don't waste them on me. Remember, you are the Instrument, but *I* am the Guide."

I nodded silently, and the Panther faded away slowly, his eyes still holding my gaze as he disappeared.

I hastily drew the Reiki distance symbol in the air and focused on the client's face that the Panther had shown me. Almost immediately, my vision zoomed in on his torso, and I saw a pulsing red "slash" of pain in his chest. As I sent emotional healing to the area, I could see what appeared to be heart valve damage, and the heart started to palpitate as I watched. Quickly, I sent my own energy to calm the palpitations, and then I drew external healing energy through his Crown chakra and down into the heart. I could see his blood pressure going down and the stress on his heart subsiding. For some unexplained reason, the symbols I received indicated that I might have just prevented a heart attack.

Quietly, I disconnected my mental link and closed my chakras. For a few moments, I just stared ahead blankly, trying to process what had just happened; I was still driving. The Panther reappeared, his face calm and reserved, and he asked me how I felt.

Without realizing it, my eyes had started to well up with tears. As one tear ran down my cheek, I softly uttered, "So THAT is unconditional love in Reiki: healing just because the person needs it..." True selflessness was sending healing and emotional relief to someone who would never know my intentions - and certainly would refuse anything at all from me if they *were* known - simply because the person was in need of help.

The Panther nodded once and then faded away. As his image dissolved, he mentally reminded me of the most powerful tenets of Reiki that I had conveniently left out of the list I had built to reject his request:

Just for today, I will not worry.

Just for today, I will not anger.

Just for today, I will be kind to every living creature.

Just for today, I will count my many blessings.

Just for today, I will do my work honestly.

Even now, as I describe this experience, I relive some of the humility and awe and hope I went through during the lesson I was given. When I tell the story, I almost always feel the tears forming in my eyes as I feel that overwhelming feeling of peace once more. It has become a source of strength to power my own self-healing in times of doubt or confusion; this is the truth of Reiki.

Chapter 6: "Natural" Energy

As I think about that day that my perspective was first changed to view these new abilities of energy healing as gifts, I have to remind myself that I was still searching for the "how" and the "why" of these ESP messages. In spite of his excessive eye-rolling, the Panther has come to terms with the idea that try as he may, he can't talk me out of classifying my evolution in my own way. The search for analytical answers has provided some interesting insights, although I must admit it has brought more questions than answers. At least we both agree that I keep testing and evaluating because I am getting pretty impressive results.

I'm sure you can see how these unexplainable experiences would give me a certain level of excitement, even while wrestling with how crazy my stories must sound. The repeatability of the procedures I practiced and the amazing results I received made me want to try more experimentation. It started to become an invigorating cycle; I would experiment during a Reiki session, and I received confirmed healing results and verified historical visions, driving my desire to try my energy reading process out again in new ways. I spent every night of the first months of my Reiki exploration training myself to view people's energy imbalances while practicing distance healing. I practiced on family members, friends, and even people who were recommended to me due to their maladies. I didn't purposefully intend to expand my experiences beyond people, but I can say that I have also received visions about and performed Reiki healing on several animals, both in person and via the distance symbol. The energy imbalances can be just the same in animals. I saw physical pain and emotional distress in the animals I worked on, but I haven't yet figured out why there seem to be differences in the way I am shown their energy fields. Sometimes, opportunity presents itself in unexpected ways.

I assume my love of animals has helped my sensitivity to their energies, and I have been around them for a large part of my life. The connections people have with their pets are usually strong, but I never anticipated that these links could be leveraged to read the animal's energy remotely. With the distance symbol, the Reiki healer can direct soothing energy across vast distances and back and forth through time, but my first animal evaluations seemed to travel "through" the animal's owners. The effort took a surprising amount of my own energy, draining me for several minutes. My most effective process was to project my sensitivity into the owner, find the connection "thread" by which the owner's emotions were attached to the animal, and then "travel down" the thread to examine the animal's energy. The animal's energy would appear over the owner's left shoulder, on a separate visual "screen" of its own. However, after the first time I identified an animal's energy, I could reconnect with it in the future without having to connect through the owner's energy. For one animal in particular, I've reached out and sent healing at least four times over the past several months; even if I am still learning to read equine energy, it's fascinating to "see" how a horse can be high-strung and emotional, affecting its own health.

Colic in a horse is quite dangerous, although it is more a symptom than a diagnosis. This abdominal pain and gas can be fatal, as it is often attributed to gastrointestinal blockages or abnormalities. Another explanation for colic is that the horse is upset and feeling a good deal of stress, introducing digestive issues, and this hints at a relationship between the emotional state of the animal and the effects of the corresponding negative energy. Stress in a person causes issues like indigestion, increased stomach acid, irritable bowel syndrome (IBS), and other abdominal problems, so why not in a horse? The horse I worked on demonstrated that it could be as stressed out as its owner, and that is saying something.

The first time I examined this horse, the horse and its owner were both far away, with thousands of miles separating us. The owner contacted me to tell me that the horse was in distress at that immediate time. The horse had gone through surgery in the recent past due an intestinal blockage, so there was a medical history of issues. At the time of the phone call, the horse was lying down because of the pain and intestinal pressure, but I had never attempted to connect with this kind of energy before. Thanks to the Panther, I learned that I didn't have to be in front of the horse to assess the animal's energy; in my mental vision of the owner, I saw a lavender "cord" leading away from the owner's Heart chakra, and the Panther's emerald eyes appeared and flashed as I studied the cord. This was the emotional connection down which I projected my sensitivity to examine the horse. I had to focus harder than normal as I separated the owner's emotions from the horse's energy review. Perhaps this cord is part of the emotional bond between the pet and its owner. Most people will agree that our pets become a "part of the family," with love and caring being sent in both directions down this connection. Another theory I have is that the connection is strong because a pet is almost fully dependent upon its owner; the health and well-being of a pet is directly linked to the owner's actions, so perhaps the dependency imparts lingering emotional "hooks" that can be traced from the owner. In my case, following the cord from the owner to the horse, I first had to isolate the equine energy, and then it took a minute or two for me to scan the horse's body.

The horse's energy was somewhat alien at first, a pale lavender in color, but I soon saw a telltale red "slash" of pain on the horse's right side, just in front of the hind leg. The red overlay went down to his underbelly, showing current distress as well as an existing scar. (Remember, the horse did have surgery in the recent past to deal with a blockage.) The pressure of an existing partial blockage of the large intestine was shown to me. It was quite painful, discomfort at a juncture of the intestine that was operated on during the procedure. The surgery to reclose the intestine and the subsequent scarring had formed a large pocket like a receptacle that allowed the collection of gas and waste in that spot. By following the energy of the reddish-hued pain through the horse's abdomen, I saw the main issue was that this intestinal "fold" had collected waste, yet the surgery had weakened the muscles around it. The muscles were having trouble contracting enough to move the blockage along the intestinal tract. As I sent my intention to try and release the blockage, I could "see" the lavender color become even lighter as I willed for the intestinal muscles to relax. I wasn't looking for it, but I could see a thin red line leading from the horse's intestine to its heart. I drew the emotion symbol in the air and directed it toward the animal over 2000 miles away. After about ten minutes of trying to soothe the abdominal swelling, my vision showed me that the intestinal muscles were kneading more effectively, and I sensed that the horse was relaxing more. In about an hour, the owner informed me that the horse was up and walking around, and the blockage had passed.

Over the course of a few months, I sent distance healing to this highly emotional horse several times, and I found that it was becoming easier to connect to his specific energy remotely. During the most recent colic episode, the horse experienced acute discomfort and was found lying down in his paddock, writhing in pain. The owner contacted me again, begging me to send Reiki relief. I opened my chakras, shielded myself, and sent my healing intention to the stricken animal by casting my energy into the air. When I connected to the horse this time, I felt an emotional change in the horse as soon as my energy connected with its lavender hue. I chuckled out loud when my extra-sensory perception told me that the horse actually recognized my remote "touch," shivering in anticipation. Had the horse learned the sensation of my remote healing contact from my previous Reiki work? I found the cause of the pain, another blockage spot, within moments, and I started "prodding" the intestinal muscles into contracting, reducing the pent-up gas pressure and breaking up the blockage. I smiled outwardly when I "saw" the intestine walls relax and push things forward. I contacted the owner and said that I saw the horse feeling better, and I found out that the horse was trotting around the paddock within five minutes of my phone call. (The Panther and I both know this won't be the last time this horse will need healing, especially seeing how closely the owner and horse are linked emotionally...)

Most of my work on other animals has been upon request. For example, I have had visions of maladies in dogs - two sisters, as a matter of fact. The owner of one of the sisters was beginning to relate how sick the dogs were, and an overlapping vision of two dogs' heads appeared over the owner's left shoulder. There was a thin, red cord of energy connecting the owner's aura to one of the canine faces, tethering the owner and pet together in an emotional bond. Over the span of about five seconds, I received a series of images "through" the owner, showing pain and swelling in both dogs' mouths and stomachs. The intuitions that flowed with the images "told" me that some type of parasitic virus had infected the gastrointestinal tracts of both dogs, contracted through food that both had shared. I could also see that one dog was sicker than the other, with a wider dissemination of tiny red dots that resembled pock marks lingering in its energy field. The owner confirmed that my reading was correct for the both the illness and how it had spread more through one sister than the other. Following the emotional cord from the owner to the pet that was still in place, I sent healing to the owner's dog. Then, in an even more tiring effort, I "hopped" from the owner's dog to her sister. I sent my intention to stop the spread of the virus internally and soothe some of the damage and pain they were experiencing. I continued to send some healing over the next few days to help both dogs fight off the virus, and I was happy to hear that they were back to their old selves quickly.

I agree with the general belief that the sensitivity of animals is pretty strong. Animals can sense changes in their environment much more effectively than humans, and I have observed this in my Reiki work. During one session, my soothing energy seemed to affect the house cat as well, even though I didn't actually intend to read or heal the cat. He appeared to take advantage of the ambient energy that I created for the actual recipient. This was a challenging session, and the changes in both client and cat were palpable, so perhaps the intensity of the available energy was strong enough to affect the cat. My client had asked me if I might help her after I shared some of my other Reiki stories with her. When she was ready, I began to comb through her energy, and I could see a large amount of negative energy attached to a still-open scar in her energy field. In her Crown chakra, there were deep pits of ashy charcoal, preventing her from being able to accept an infusion of universal healing. Moving lower, I received glimpses of her Heart chakra, spinning very slowly because it was partially filled with a thick, black paste, but I could move it around to get the chakra energy spinning when I tried. As I attempted to remove some of the paste, another challenge was presented to me: a thin plate of obsidian appeared in her neck, as if a sheet of black metal had slid through the front of her neck and out of the back, effectively separating the head from the torso like in a magician's trick. I had never seen anything like this before, and for some reason, I could not remove the sheet. Instead of removing it, I decided to focus my intention into a sharp instrument to punch metaphysical "holes" in the sheet so that energy would be able to flow through it, allowing energy to go back and forth between the Crown and Heart chakras. Another unexpected challenge was that the negative charcoal in her Crown chakra replenished itself while I was working to remove it. Following my instincts, I asked the Panther to help me clear the Crown chakra, and he was able to use his powerful claws to "dig through" the layer of ash so that I could guide healing energy into the top of her head. Once the healing energy was inside, I moved it down through the pierced holes in the obsidian plate to reach the Heart chakra.

Now enter the cat. When I started the Reiki session, the cat was playing with anything it could find. It would run around, swat at a string, the curtains, a newspaper, or even a chair leg, play with a feather toy, and charge into another room. I could hear all of this commotion, but I tuned it out when I started viewing the depth of the work ahead of me. I stopped around fifteen minutes into the Reiki session to describe one of the visions I had just seen to my client when my senses realized I didn't hear the pitter-patter of the cat running around anymore. I asked,

"Where's the cat?" We both looked around but didn't see it...until I looked under the couch that my client was laying on. There was the cat, slowly walking back and forth under the couch lengthwise. Each time it would come out from under the end of the couch, it would look up and right into my eyes for a moment, turn around, and go back to stroll under the couch in the other direction. The cat did this at least three times while I was watching, and my senses told me it kept going beyond that. I resumed the Reiki session, working negative energy out of her feet, until I paused for another explanation. Once again, the cat was out of sight. "Now where is he?" We found the cat asleep. It has climbed into a chair, curled up, and drifted off for a nap. My client said, "I've never seen that cat in that chair. He doesn't go to sleep until 1 am," and it was only 10:40 pm. As soon as the Reiki session was over, the cat jumped down from the chair, crossed back into the room we were in, and laid down at the base of the couch. Did the cat actually respond to the universal healing energy I had channeled into the room?

The emotional and physical states of animals were intriguing to see, and the insights into following emotional "cords" from one subject to another showed me things that I didn't anticipate on my own. As I received one Reiki insight, another would follow, my intentions on broadening my energy "horizon" were no exception. Accepting for a moment that the human body is made up of spiritual and physical energy, it is recognized that animals, plants, and even the planet have physical energy, but are there spiritual energies as well? An inexplicable intuition found me a new way to test out my energy reading skills. My own scientific curiosity and background helped me identify a new source of natural energy to examine: geomagnetic energy. Could I extend my sensitivity to energies in the world around me?

At the time, it seemed like a valid hypothesis, looking at the energies in living creatures. The brain transmits electrical energy to the body's muscles to impel them into action; this electrical energy also generates a weak magnetic field, which can be detected and measured. There is also a great deal of electromagnetic energy to be found within the Earth itself. The Earth generates a magnetic field, from the core of the planet to the ionized solar winds emanating from the Sun. The field fluctuates and moves slowly as masses of molten iron and alloys shift around in the core of the planet. There are locations on the Earth's surface at which these magnetic fields can be observed. As I mulled over the challenge of how I might attune myself to natural magnetic energy, an idea popped into my head: "Of course! I have family in Arizona! What better way to expose myself to natural magnetic fields than to visit the famous vortexes outside of the city of Sedona?!" (The tourist culture there calls them "vortexes," not "vortices.") I immediately called my family and told them of my interest to check out the vortexes, and they were happy to go. Even if you don't have any experiences around the vortexes, the countryside outside of Sedona is truly beautiful, but I was using this trip as an experiment. I had been to these places before, so I had a series of "control" experiences to use. On my previous trips to these Sedona spots where people allege there are energies flowing up out of the ground, I had felt nothing - no tingling, no disorientation, not even a temperature fluctuation. I was convinced that these were just superstitious beliefs derived from rumors and tales from the region dating back centuries. Thinking back on my decision to revisit these locations, I'm proud of myself for looking beyond my lack of previous experiences and trying again to sense these energies. In effect, I formed a new test scenario that included the variable of my new-found Reiki sensitivity. However, my research prior to the trip couldn't scientifically confirm the existence of geomagnetic energy in these spots, so I had no idea what to expect.

The first stop outside of downtown Sedona was the Boynton Canyon vortex site. After looking into the locations online, I chose Boynton Canyon because there were supposed to be two vortexes within 100 yards of each other up on a hill. One vortex was supposed to flow in a counterclockwise direction (the "male" vortex), and the other flowed in a clockwise direction (the "female" counterpart). I didn't sense a "male" or "female" component in either energy field, but the directions of the energy flows were significant. The general practice of Reiki teaches that manipulating the chakras and other energy fields in a clockwise fashion is performed to absorb energy into the body through the chakra node.

Directing the chakra to rotate in a counterclockwise direction is meant to radiate energy out from the chakra or reduce the energy intake of the node. This directional difference also applies to my drawing of the physical healing symbol; I draw it in the air as a counterclockwise pattern while I am sending energy to my client. With the opportunity to experience both energy types, I was looking forward to getting to the state park.

However, when I arrived at the park, my mental state was anything but calm. Another note to self: make sure you don't eat cheese-filled mushrooms, even unwittingly, before going to a national park when you are lactose-intolerant; it doesn't go well. After dealing with the consequences, I grumpily tromped up the trail to get to the hilltop that my family had already reached. At the edge of the hilltop, there was a cool natural spire. I noticed how this rock formation looked a bit like an alligator-headed hard candy dispenser. As I reflected upon this funny imagery, I released my frustration and stopped trying to force my energy interaction. I approached the spot where the counterclockwise energy vortex was supposed to be but felt nothing at all. This long drive, the bad dairy reaction, the hike up the hill - all for nothing. I folded my arms and shook my head in disgust, "What a waste...of...whoa..."

My intuitive senses shifted my perception subconsciously to seek out a tingly energy I felt at the edge of my senses. My clairvoyant sensitivity showed me an amazing sight: I was standing inside an energy tornado formed by swirling black particles, rotating around me and creating the perimeter of the geyser of energy. The path of each particle orbiting around me left a thin, black line in its wake, effectively outlining the morphing shape of the spinning vortex that went up at least 50 feet in the air. I was in the eye of the vortex, and I could see how my own personal energy, also radiating out from me in a counterclockwise direction, was interacting with the wall of the funnel, each field drawing strength from the other in a synergistic way. The world around me started to spin as well, making me disoriented until I grounded myself and broke contact with the vortex. When things had settled down, I realized my family was staring at me with slightly worried expressions. I told them I was fine, and I started to describe what I had just seen and felt...but it was only the beginning.

Telling my story of the spinning tornado amplifying my own energy, I studied my family's faces. They were supportive of this Reiki journey I was on, yet my reactions to the vortex took them by surprise. Most of them sat down on the rocks in the area of the vortex as they listened to me. At the edge of my senses, I noticed something about each of them, so I let my perception shift back to match the vortex energy, and I could see small cords of energy reaching up out of the rocks to connect with each of them. While we talked, I had each person shift in place or move to a different rock to connect better with the energy radiating from the rock face. They could feel the energy vibration in the rock once they were positioned "correctly," and they manipulated it in different ways. One formed a mini vortex within her cupped hands, and she was pulled down toward the rocks until she broke the grip. Another could run her hands across the rocks and sense different levels of vibrations. A third absorbed energy from the rocks with his right hand, but he didn't release it; I watched it build up within him, and he kept absorbing more. I told him to get up and move to the base of the rocks and then sit back down to help drain the energy out of him into the ground.

While most of my family sat down, one remained standing, arms folded and totally uninterested in feeling any energy at all. "You're all crazy! Forget all this 'feeling' and 'seeing' crap; I'm gonna go look at the trees and cool rocks; they're pretty..." This was not an unexpected response. This person was still supportive of my Reiki evolution but wanted nothing to do with experiencing things for herself. It wasn't the comment that stopped me in my tracks and made me laugh out loud; it was the vision of the vortex swirling around her that surprised me. I still saw the vortex lines swirling around me, and she stood within the wall of the energy tornado, except that the lines of energy would not pass through her. I could see the vortex lines approach her right shoulder in the same counterclockwise paths, the particles coming within four inches of her, but then completely changing course to soar up and over her head in an arc, maintaining the four-inch distance away from her, coming back down toward the left shoulder and then resuming its circular course around me, just to swerve around her again in the same soaring arc. When I realized that I could see four particles soaring over her in equidistant arcs, I couldn't help but laugh! The "stubbornness" of this person to NOT experience any energy seemed to form a personal shield around her, forcing the swirling energy particles to flow around the shield and resume their natural course on the other side. (I enjoy the fact that even though she still maintains that she doesn't want to have any experiences with energy, natural or otherwise, she has found reasons to tell this story of "shielding" herself from the energy many times, laughing at what these bending energy waves must have looked like. Remember, she never actually SAW any of these bands of energy...)

Right after I saw the bending waves of energy being "forced" around her, another visitor to the vortex, a stranger, approached the rocks. She had overheard my conversation and instructions to my family as I guided them to different locations, and she jokingly said, "What about me? Where should I sit?" I chuckled, saying, "Well, I don't know how...I..." But once again, I shifted my perception to see a spot where her energy would match that of the vortex. I had her climb up a few rocks, move over to the right, and sit down. She followed my instructions and then said, "OK, what am I supposed to...feel...whoa, what IS that?!" She had a far-off look for several moments before I climbed down off the rocks. Turning back, I said to her, "See what I mean?"

At this point, I decided to walk over to the other nearby vortex. Some people believe that the Boynton Canyon vortexes are actually two parts of the same vortex. For me, they are two separate vortexes with different rotational directions and different properties. Walking across the hilltop, I got within fifty feet of the location of the other energy well and began to feel very strange. The first words I uttered were, "Oh man...this is...chaotic..." I was disoriented, unable to focus my thoughts, until I readjusted my perceptions. Suddenly, I could see two separate energy fields, one coming from my own counterclockwise energy and the other swirling in a wider, clockwise storm. The particles from my energy crashed into and collided with those of the vortex, flying off in random directions and disappearing. As I approached the spot where the center of the vortex was supposed to be, the collisions became more violent. I couldn't explain why, but I didn't feel...right...during this "assault" on my energy, and I found myself saying "no" out loud. In response, I half-consciously raised my own Reiki shield to protect me from...whatever...this energy was. I immediately felt better, and I could see some of the vortex lines crash against my shield of white light. My family saw my discomfort and asked me if I wanted to leave, but my instincts told me that I should stay and experience this energy source that seemed to flow opposite to my own.

For the rest of my time in Boynton Canyon, I could feel the "pressure" of the clockwise vortex, pounding away at my shield, but the strength and resilience of my shield were exceptional. Finally, we started descending the trail back to the parking lot. While talking with my sister, I continued to experience the sensation of a vacuum against my shield, the clockwise vortex attempting to drain my energy, almost as if it had recognized me. Halfway down the hill, I decided to drop my shield and open myself to the vortex. Almost instantly, I felt my energy reserves being sucked out of my hands back toward the hilltop. It almost brought me to my knees, so I quickly raised my personal shield and grounded my energy. The pull of the vortex ended as soon as my shield was up again. I felt the buffeting of the vortex against my shield all the way back to the car.

To end the day in Sedona, we traveled to the Red Rock Crossing/Cathedral Rock vortex, about 30 minutes from Boynton Canyon. When we got out of the car, I remembered that I had my attuned Reiki crystals with me. I asked myself which crystal would be "associated" with the vortex once we reached it. I pulled each crystal out of my pocket in one by one. When the emotion crystal was drawn, it was already warm, while the others were cool. I decided to carry this crystal in my hand as I approached the reported location of the vortex. Actually, I wasn't quite sure of the exact location from the rough map I had. When I got within "range" of the vortex, I didn't see it, but I could sense the size and strength of its counterclockwise spin, parallel to the ground. It was like a three-bladed turbine, maybe 50 yards across or more, and I felt the calm power of each blade as it moved past me, one every few seconds: "fwoom, fwoom, fwoom." The intensity of the energy grew as I walked upstream, seeking the center of the vortex, until I felt it in the middle of the river at the base of a cliff wall of red rock. It was a tranquil, soothing energy, relaxing and revitalizing me as I sat on the riverbank.

During the ride home, I reflected upon my strange experiences, but it wasn't until weeks later that I decided that these were learning opportunities: 1) I had learned the sensation, and to some degree, the initiation of combining my energy with an additive one; and 2) I learned the protective strength of my personal shield against subtractive energy or draining energy sinks. These discoveries were to become very important to my future sensitivity development. I didn't anticipate what that future sensitivity would be, but more on that later; the week wasn't finished yet.

Chapter 7: The Declaration

After seeing and feeling the diverse energies of multiple vortexes in Sedona, I was feeling good about the "progress" I had made with my growing sensitivity, but that was only the first day of the vacation. The week of visiting my family did not end with the vortex experiences; the remaining time was full of amazing experiences along with a few radical realizations that I didn't always interpret as positive. My reactions to these events were mixed, and my conflicting emotions made it even harder to analyze the realizations and their implications logically. My attempts to categorize the intuitions I received were overwhelmed at times by a sense of confusion or even fear. However, no matter how challenging it was to go through these events, the resulting spiritual evolution I have experienced was worth it. Even now, I am still learning things about myself now that I touched on back then.

The visions of the swirling particle trails of the Sedona vortexes are experiences I will never forget. I felt as though my sensitivity became stronger after seeing these surging tornadoes, and I was ready to look for new opportunities to test my senses. Thinking back about the events of that week, though, I now understand just how limited my views were about the scope of my sensitivity. I also realized months later that my lack of understanding was self-imposed to a certain degree; there were things I didn't comprehend because part of me didn't want to face the consequences of accepting them, although I continued to apply my sensitivity theories based on energy conservation to many experiences I had. Even though I used the notion of energy transforming into new forms in order to explain what I saw and felt, my conscious mind never linked one type of energy sensitivity to another. The Panther didn't nudge me in a direction, either, so I was on my own to develop an explanation for what was happening to me.

I should probably comment on my interest in the paranormal at this point. For many years, I have been a fan of the television shows that helped move the practice of ghost hunting more deeply into our mainstream culture. One of the things I appreciate about them is that they are based upon collecting evidence. There are so many different opinions about the existence of paranormal phenomena; some people embrace the idea of separate planes of existence through which the spirit travels, while others guarantee that a rational explanation can be found for every event. Before my spiritual journey, I was a believer in the paranormal, but there were caveats to my accepting the existence of ghostly activity. First and foremost, the work of alleged spirit mediums didn't really add to my belief. It's not that I didn't believe in mediumship; many people have a certain sensitivity to various frequencies of energy, and I always felt that some people could become attuned to spiritual energy as well. My problem with mediums was that I didn't want to base my perspectives upon the "feelings" or sensations experienced by someone else. A medium telling me that a ghost is walking the halls of an old sanitarium doesn't really do ME any good; how am I supposed to know it is true? The paranormal TV shows I watched intended to compile physical evidence to support claims of hauntings. (There will be people that argue that the shows contrived all of their evidence, and nothing anyone says will change their minds...and I have to agree that with some of the interactions I have heard about with these TV crews, I have some doubts of my own.) The allure for me has been the collection of recorded evidence that can be shared with people who have never even visited the location. Hearing a recording, capturing an image, and showing a temperature change are ways to introduce experiences to anyone who wishes to check them out, and they don't rely on someone else's senses or intuitions. If you accept the integrity of the investigating group, they can sometimes show you some pretty remarkable events, and you can capture your own evidence if you wish. For me, seeing and hearing these events myself are critical to my accepting an event being classified as paranormal.

The city of Tombstone, Arizona, is about an hour east of Tucson by car, and it is reputed to be a very haunted town. There are several locations in town that host ghost tours, and the locals maintain that spirits walk the streets at night. Since it sounded like a fun day trip, I set up a ghost tour reservation at one of the "hottest" paranormal spots in Tombstone, and I stayed in a motel that was reportedly haunted as well. Members of my family traveled with me to join me on the tour. The ghost tour we joined in this famous landmark was interesting; the place has a well-known history, and famous Tombstone celebrities, like Wyatt Earp, his brothers Virgil and Morgan, Doc Holliday, Curly Bill Brocius, Johnny Ringo, and many others were supposed to frequent the shows held there.

The tour itself was split in two, with a lights-on walk through the location and then an extended lights-out session with the guests sitting in the dark. The lights-out session was held with a "spirit box," a frequency-hopping FM-band device through which ghosts are supposed to be able to communicate verbally by manipulating the frequency scans. My family and I thought we heard a few words and a cowboy's name "Dex" come through the spirit box, but the sounds were usually hard to understand. At the end of the tour, the lights were turned back on, and I was looking around the place. I stood peering through the slats in an old wooden door that led up to a landing. When I looked to the end of the landing, my heart skipped a beat - a black shadow in the shape of a cowboy boot with a spur attached to it moved from the lighted area on the right side of the landing and into some chamber on the left side! My jaw dropped, and a wave of chills washed over me. When my family called out to me, they saw me transfixed while facing the door: "You about ready to go? I think we...did you just SEE something?!" That was the first time I had ever witnessed what I believe was a shadow person; I never observed a paranormal phenomenon first-hand before (or, at least I never recognized one before).

I was really excited about seeing that shadow, even though it lasted only an instant. When we left the building, my family and I were rehashing the events of the lights-out session, and I couldn't stop talking about the boot shadow. We were walking down the street when we saw a pair of guests from our tour going into another building, and we overheard that this place was also hosting a ghost tour. I was invigorated by the previous tour, so I convinced my family to join me inside this building, in spite of the fact that it didn't have a sign outside. (Since then, the history of the building has been researched, and the new sign says "Watt & Tarbell, Undertakers" outside of the building on Allen Street[6]...) As soon as we walked inside and met the sisters who run the tours, I knew this was going to be a memorable event, as a twist-top flashlight laying on the circular table at the front of the room was turning on and off all by itself! Stacy and Nora of Sister Paranormal Investigators, or SPI[7], have been hosting the ghost tours in the mortuary since February, 2014. They began the tour with a history of the building, but I admit I missed a lot of it because I was focused on the flashlight's random activation with no one near the table. The tour took us throughout the building, passing the old bar area, into the rear storage area, and even down to a tunnel beneath the building used by immigrants in the 1800s to travel unseen throughout the town. After touring the building, we all sat down at the circular table, which had several meters for recording temperature, audio, and electromagnetic fields on it...and the flashlight was still lighting up on its own. Soon, the sisters turned off the lights in the building, and the place came alive, no pun intended...

The session started with the sisters' spirit box turned off. Stacy and Nora began to ask questions to the building, and we started hearing knocks on the wall and hard-heeled footsteps on the floorboards near the front of the room. They would ask the "spectral visitors" to answer simple questions by turning the flashlight on or off, or by moving closer to set off the electromagnetic meter on the table. Stacy demonstrated to the tour how taking flash photography with a smartphone during the lights-out session could sometimes result in capturing light reflections from free-floating energy orbs. Orbs like these have been theorized to provide evidence of paranormal potential energy, as the spherical energy masses would be the easiest form of energy for an entity to manipulate. (It should be noted that orbs can be found in nature; the existence of floating spheres of energy does not necessarily indicate evidence of spirits or paranormal energy.) The tour guests took their own pictures all night long, and in many of the images, orbs having a variety of sizes and shapes were captured. With orbs being observed right on top of the flashlight, credence grew for the explanation that spirits were interacting with it and causing it to dim or brighten upon request. Nora, who, I am now convinced, is a gifted medium, pointed out locations of shadow figures and orbs and told the tour guests where and when to take their own pictures. Then the FM-hopping spirit box was connected to a set of speakers and turned on. The tour guests began to ask questions...and hear responses.

The spirit box communication was incredible, with the local "residents" of the mortuary providing their names, like Adam, Peter, Steve, Bill, and Anna. Each response was in a different voice, adding to the idea that there were many spirits lingering around the building. Questions about these names were "confirmed" by the flashlights being turned on and off. It's important to note here that I brought my own flashlight to the tour, and it was being manipulated as well, so the activity was validated. As the sisters asked more complex questions, the responses were even more incredible. Here are some of the results from the question-and-answer session:

Q. "Is someone touching my hair right now?"

A. "Touched you..."

Q. "Does anyone have a plan for robbing the bank and stealing all of the silver?"

A. "Absolutely."

Q. "Do you like my silver earrings?"

A. "Sure."

Q. "Where are you from?"

A. "Tombstone."

Q. "How are you doing today?"

A. "Good."

Q. "Is there someone blowing on the back of my neck?"

A. "Yes."

That last example is significant in many ways, but especially because the question came from ME. Earlier in the evening, Stacy made an announcement to the female spirit "residents" in the building that there were handsome gentlemen at the table, and she wondered out loud if one of us might like to have his hair touched or have one of them blow on his neck. I immediately volunteered: "Oh, I would!" I didn't think much of it, even when a woman's voice said through the spirit box, "I will..." I was recording the investigation using both a digital audio recorder and a night vision camcorder, and I was trying to capture any anomalies on video, so I wasn't paying attention to my immediate surroundings. While I was zooming in on the mirror mounted on the shelf behind the bar, I started to notice a distinctive drop in temperature on my left elbow. It was distracting enough for me to look down from the camcorder screen and mention the phenomenon to the tour group.

Suddenly, I started to feel a chill go down my spine, as a faint draft blew across the left side of my neck. As I prepared to describe this draft to everyone else, the wind became stronger, more forceful, and much colder. It was as if someone was standing to the left of me, over my shoulder, and the person put a few ice cubes in his mouth and started to blow on my neck. The intense cold air went on for about 60 seconds;

I sat back in awe as the icy wind continued to strike me. Just before it disappeared, I asked my sister to get up and come over to where I was sitting to confirm that she felt it. Unfortunately, the wind died before she reached me, which was frustrating, since I wanted independent confirmation of the experience. After that amazing event, I never would have guessed that about fifteen minutes later, the icy breath would return, stronger than before. This time, the frosty breeze was directed at my cheek and ear, and the air flow was wide enough to blow past my nose. It was a constant pressure, and it was strong enough as it blew past me that my sister could feel it on her outstretched hand while she sat about five feet away. The icy breath was colder, more intense than during the previous event. I moved my chair into a new position, rotating it to a new angle with respect to the central table, and this frigid breeze moved in sync with me to continue to blow forcefully on my cheek! I was amazed. If I hadn't been experiencing it myself, it would have been hard for me to believe. It wasn't a scary event, either; I was enjoying the paranormal event too much to consider any potential consequences. The scary event for me, the true revelation, came later on the tour.

After the chilling wind died down, I was exhilarated. As far as I could tell, that was my first direct contact with a spirit entity, and the confirmation from my sister that she experienced it as well made it even more incredible. The lights-out investigation went on, and the flashlight confirmations continued to impress everyone. Unfortunately, I didn't catch a glimpse of any of the shadows that the sisters pointed out (not on THIS visit, anyway). Toward the end of the tour, the interactive spirit box conversations became more infrequent, but that didn't change the amazement we all felt. At one point, Nora was pointing out that she felt something lifting her hair from behind her chair. Out of the blue, she surprised me by looking straight at me and said, "You saw that, didn't you? You saw that orb, right?" What surprised me even more was that I knew what she was talking about. We were still sitting in the dark, yet there was a fading image in my field of vision that resembled the lingering "burned-in" remnants of an intense flash of sparking light. (I compare this to looking at the sun quickly, and then closing your eyes;

you can still see the dim after-images of light as they begin to fade.) I wasn't even sure what I was seeing as I focused on this dim image of multiple sparks of light. My response was, "Is THAT what I just saw?" Nora tilted her head and looked appraisingly at me for a moment, and then she made what I later dubbed The Declaration that shook me to my core: "You are a sensitive, and you are in denial."

Immediately after her revelation, I had a physical reaction for which I coined another phrase related to my growing sensitivity: the Chills of Truth. When she told me she thought I was a sensitive, a deep, rippling series of chills started in the middle of my chest and moved simultaneously up toward my head and down toward my feet. My body trembled all over, and I almost collapsed. I bent over and dropped my head into my hands down between my knees. I mumbled, "No, no, no, don't tell me that..." The trembling chills told me without a doubt that she was right, and an extensive series of thoughts and images flowed through my mind over only a few moments that argued against any denial I could make. How could I actually see the Sedona vortexes if I wasn't a sensitive? Where in my Reiki training did it describe seeing floating, sparking orbs with the naked eye? I told myself as I worked to evolve my Reiki skills that my visions and energy readings about people's histories were just a normal part of my Reiki healing, because it was easier to accept this than to wrestle with more metaphysical reasons behind my gifts. I was already having enough trouble with the scientific explanations of energy healing; I had spent the last few months deceiving myself that I could classify all of those events that I had experienced within the single scope of Reiki.

I was utterly overwhelmed...and a little afraid. Unfortunately, I couldn't put into words exactly what I was afraid of. Nora's next statement heightened my fear: "You need to take it seriously, and you need to protect yourself." She went on to talk about her experience with both good and evil entities, and she wanted to make sure that I carefully considered the possible consequences of my future actions. (Oh great; now I felt LOADS better...) My head was still in my hands when Nora stood up and walked over to me. She guided me to stand up, and she wrapped her arms around me in a hug, telling me to be strong. After the tour was over, my family and I sat and talked with the sisters for another two hours, listening to their experiences in the mortuary over the past month, discussing my recent Reiki readings, and promising we would be back. (In the months to come, we returned several times, and now the paranormal activity in the Watt & Tarbell mortuary will be the source of a new documentary being compiled at the time of this writing...)

Her warnings continue to reverberate in my mind: Be strong? Protect myself? From what?! These questions weren't really the source of my fear. The cold stab of fear in my gut was hard to define, but it was very real. It took me some time to recognize how my respect for the paranormal led me to be afraid of unanticipated outcomes of any paranormal experimentation. I feared the possibility that I might unleash some unknown power that I wouldn't recognize or couldn't control. It was a real possibility to me, and I wasn't actually worried for my own welfare; I was worried what my novice experimentation might do to the people around me. My reaction to this realization was not to promise myself to be careful and learn all I can to avoid any issues. Instead, I retreated inside myself. I didn't want to talk about my experiences. I didn't even want to talk about Reiki healing. I shut that part of my mind down for the time being, and I focused on the fun of the tours. By the next morning, I was back to my old self again, but with a mental barrier in place that wasn't ready to revisit what had happened.

It probably didn't help my attitude that I didn't get much sleep that night, because my hotel room was haunted. After the tour, we returned to the hotel, and I had a room all to myself...except that I wasn't alone. The other "guest" in my room spent hours knocking on the inner wall of the room that led to the bathroom. It was pretty shocking, and I was scared the first time I heard the changing pitch of the knocking as it moved down the wall. Right after the knocking stopped, I heard the thud of footsteps on the ceiling of the building. (Years ago, there was a second floor to this building, which served as a bordello, but the building was now only a single story.) I started to panic, hiding under the covers at the first series of knocking, but then I caught myself: wait a minute-why was I scared?! This was the reason I wanted to be in a haunted hotel room in the first place! From then on, I enjoyed every episode of the knocking and footsteps. In fact, it got to the point where my guest seemed to knock whenever I had just fallen back to sleep. Foolishly, I didn't turn on any of my equipment to capture this evidence. I kept threatening to turn on my camcorder, yet the bangs and thumps continued. Finally, I made good on my threat, but the knocking stopped for the rest of the night, as if my guest was aware of my attempts to record its existence.

We took the sisters and some of their family members out for brunch the next day; in that one evening of paranormal events and revelations, we had become like an extended family. No one mentioned the Declaration that day, and I was more than happy not to be reminded of it. The drive back to my parents' house passed pretty quickly, and we spent most of the trip recounting the spirit activity from the night before. However, when I got back to the house, I found out that my sister had shared the Declaration with a family friend, Angela, who was interested in the paranormal. Angela had generously given me an interesting book to read, as it helped her explore her own sensitivity. At that point, I was far from grateful; I was angry. This was MY private business, and I wasn't going to talk to anyone about it. My family had no right to include other people in the discussion. Couldn't they just leave me alone right now? I was having enough trouble with the Declaration; I wasn't about to turn this into an open family discussion at the dinner table. I was so withdrawn from my energy sensitivity that I didn't want to even consider hosting a Reiki healing session for my mother, because I refused to face the "sensitive" label that I knew in the depths of my heart was true. I was in no mood to open myself up at that time, but I went through with the Reiki session the next morning. (I had to force myself into the session before I could even begin to use my clairvoyant Reiki skills, yet part of the benefit of being a Reiki healer is that I share in the healing as I direct it into my client.)

I flew back home that afternoon, and I decided to kill some time on the flight by thumbing through this unwelcome book so that I could throw it away when I got home. Halfway through the flight, I had pretty much forgotten about my self-pity. Reading the book on the plane was a bit distracting, because I kept looking around me to see if anyone was noticing my jaw dropping open at every turn of the page. The author wrote a description of known and unexplained sensitivity examples that he went through. I had gone through at least six of the events he described over the past three years! I caught myself saying out loud, "Whoa! That makes so much sense now!" and I looked around sheepishly in case someone overheard these exclamations, as I was sitting in a middle seat on the plane...not that I had any intention to stop reading, mind you. One personal event in particular was completely changed in my mind after I read the author's accounts, and this event took place months before even before my Reiki class. I was out having dinner with a friend one night, and we were walking back to my car in the parking lot of the restaurant. I had to walk around to the other side of the car to drive, but as I approached the far side, another car drove by. I wanted to see what kind of car it was, so I stopped paying attention to what I was doing. When the car passed, I finally opened the door to get in...but something wasn't quite right. Without looking up, I stared down at a piece of paper on the driver's seat. "How did that get there?" I picked it up and put in my pocket. But that wasn't the problem. I looked up at the dashboard, but the steering wheel was an opaque silhouette. I didn't understand this, and I slowly reached for it, my hand passing right through it. My friend caught my attention by saying, "Umm, what are you doing?" I looked around and saw her looking over her shoulder from the front passenger seat; I was trying to get into the car and drive from the back! When I realized what I had done, I fell across the back seat because I was laughing so hard! I was so sure that the steering wheel was in front of me! On the plane, while I was reading the book, the author described how sometimes people get in the shower and reach for the hot-water control knob, but it isn't there, even though they were certain it was exactly where they were reaching. This phenomenon was described in the book as an unconscious shift in perception, altering the impression of the area around you[8]. Is THAT what happened to me with the steering wheel?! I could actually see the steering wheel in the back seat as the frame of a three-dimensional ring. This helped me explain how my work with Reiki and shifting my perception to read energy provided insight to how I might be able to view other phenomena. (Thank you to my sister and her great friend Angela for caring enough to try and help me understand my sensitivity, in spite of me wallowing in pathetic denial. It is always a step in the right direction when you find out that you aren't alone...)

Even with my internal struggles to accept the Declaration, I finally embraced my status of being a sensitive, going beyond the Reiki intuitions and energy readings and forging into the realm of mediumship. I am forever grateful to Nora for pointing me in a new direction. I had to face myself and re-evaluate my analytical mind in a whole new way. My anger and fear were misplaced, but that didn't make them any less real. I had to go through that bout of self-pity before I could move on. (Remember, self-healing wasn't a strong suit for me...)

In a future chapter, I will provide more background on my approach to finding another training class to attend. This time, I focused on spirit energy and contact. Some pretty surprising things have come out of that course and from my practical experimentation, yet the Declaration made it all possible. With the incredible activity I sat through in Watt & Tarbell's old mortuary, I wanted to experience more and test my sensitivity with experimentation. I learned some techniques to protect myself, and I started taking new ghost tours, armed with a backpack full of technical equipment. But I still had no way to gauge my sensitivity, and I wondered how I would know when I was experiencing something paranormal. It turns out I didn't have to worry about this; the paranormal world around me didn't let me wonder for long...

Chapter 8: Acceptance

How would you go about accepting, I mean truly accepting, that after over 40 years of existence in the material world of the five senses, you discover another "world" of energy that continues to unfold in unexpected ways, using a previously unrecognized sixth sense? The definitions and physics of the material world have been documented and can be verified by empirical testing. In many demonstrations of energy in the natural world, people can see, hear, and feel the effects of the transfer of energy through events like thunder, lightning, sunlight, fire, and magnetism. Science has identified ways to categorize and measure the amount and intensity of energy in these displays. Electrical power plants, for example, illustrate the storage and transmission of electricity for commercial use. As part of the generation process, these plants often consume one type of fuel for energy, like coal, to generate another type of energy, with a measurable "conversion" rate. The law of universal energy conservation helps define the alteration of energy types: in a closed system, energy cannot be created or destroyed; it merely changes form[9]. So where does that leave spirit energy?

Where does the study of paranormal energy, existing at a frequency far higher than energies in the natural world, come in? When intention and individual perception are the "senses" required to detect the existence of spiritual energy, how do you demonstrate it? How do you measure it? How can you explain to someone else that it is nearby, when most people have not yet learned how to interact with it? In my case, I had to find my own answers to these questions, but the biggest challenge that I faced was not telling other people about my energy sensitivity; it was getting myself to accept that I was truly sensing it.

For me, I had to define the experimentation into my paranormal sensitivity by coming up with a set of repeatable procedures and some method to evaluate the corresponding results, just like I did with Reiki. This is easier said than done! I didn't even know what my "spirit alert signs" were to indicate nearby paranormal energy, so I decided to try and relate the red "slashes" of pain and the black ooze of negative energy in my Reiki readings to some type of clairvoyant symbol for paranormal energy. Once again, my logical mind tried to define the symbols I expected to receive from my interaction with paranormal events, and once again, my self-made expectations made me miss the real events when they were happening. I looked for what I thought the energy interaction *should* be, in spite of my extremely limited experience, and I overlooked the interaction that actually took place. (You might wonder why I hadn't learned my lesson to stop making these assumptions by this point; I often ask myself the same thing...)

I kicked off my experimentation by looking for signs of those after-images of light, like the sparkling "color negative" of the light orb I saw in the mortuary. I would close my eyes and search for any residual images that would imprint themselves on my sight, but I never saw anything. I maintained my respect and fear of the possibility of some unexpected consequence of my paranormal experimentation, so I would put up my Reiki shield and ground myself to ensure my own protection. Once I was secure in my own protective measures, I would then call out to any entities nearby, inviting them to show themselves or make a sound. Looking at this process, I realize I made several potentially faulty assumptions with this approach: 1) I assumed there were entities around me that would communicate upon command; 2) I assumed that they would manifest strongly enough to be seen or make a sound; and 3) I assumed I would recognize the form this energy would take if it actually manifested. I didn't let myself get too discouraged by the complete lack of paranormal energy around me, since I knew I may not have been looking for the right signs, anyway. Then something occurred to me: maybe I should try my tests again in a place that was reported to be haunted. For example, there had to be a better chance to experience paranormal activity in a place like Eastern State Penitentiary, an old prison turned museum located in Philadelphia[10], with a history of visitors reporting unexplainable events. I had seen ghost investigations take place in different cell blocks inside Eastern State Penitentiary on several paranormal TV shows. The prison's history offers good opportunities for residual paranormal energy, and it has a variety of wings and sections that take up a full city block, including Death Row, a prison hospital, an old chapel, and a synagogue.

With a friend, I visited Eastern State a few years before my Reiki class, and I was fascinated by its decrepit cell walls and its diverse prisoner population when it was an active penitentiary. We walked the halls and entered the cells, yet I didn't sense anything out of the ordinary. I did take many pictures, with three of them showing energy orbs reflecting the flash of my digital camera. My night-vision camcorder captured a disembodied scream that ended in a male voice that said, "Remember me?" I also captured a floating light anomaly in one of the cells, coming out of the wall and then disappearing near the small table in the cell. Unfortunately, I didn't see or hear any of these phenomena with my own senses on my tour of the museum, but I was excited by the evidence I had found when I reviewed what I had recorded. Then again, I hadn't actually been trying to "detect" anything during that first visit. With this growing energy sensitivity, it was time to return to the prison and put my senses to the test.

I decided to take my next tour of Eastern State Penitentiary, and I ended up going by myself. I entered the front gate and started listening to the audio guided tour. I thought that the recorded descriptions could act as background noise to let me focus on testing my second sight, but that didn't last long. It was more distracting to keep hitting "Play" and half-listen to the audio, so I went back to the front desk and turned the audio player in. I returned to the main courtyard and picked a random cell block entrance, different from the one in which the tour begins. I slowly walked down the hallway, taking pictures in any cell that caught my attention, watching the digital screen for any unexpected images or distortions. Nothing happened. After two hours and three full cell blocks' worth of pictures, I sat down on a bench and took a break. With my camera in hand, I took a look at my last seven or eight pictures, but I still didn't see any unusual images. I lowered the camera and stared into the cell in front of me as I thought about the next spot I wanted to visit...but something happened that interrupted me from picking a location. Looking through the narrow cell doorway in the wall, my attention was caught by some type of movement about halfway into the cell, on the right wall near the ceiling. The image was like a rippling of a shadow in the air, similar to the waves of heat emanating up from an asphalt road in the summer. This distortion of energy lasted just under two seconds, yet it was unmistakable: a sphere of shimmering energy lines, casting gray shadows in the air as they radiated outward from the central core of the orb. Luckily, I wasn't completely in shock, and I fumbled to raise my camera and snapped a picture. This time, when I reviewed the still image, the flash reflected off of some type of oblong energy orb floating through the air. It had what appeared to be a nucleus in the lower right area of the orb. Seeing this floating phenomenon, I quickly took several more pictures, yet there was no sign of the orb. I thought to myself, "Maybe I've just discovered a way that my sensitivity would locate paranormal energy..."

After seeing that energy distortion, I completely changed my tour activities. Instead of viewing the cells and chambers through the digital screen of my camcorder, I looked into every cell with my own eyes, letting them go in and out of focus in the hopes that shimmering waves of energy might appear again, and I wasn't disappointed. I still took a large number of pictures in locations that I didn't see any distortions, but now I was trying to follow my instincts and tap into any sensitivity messages I might receive. Over the next few hours, I saw three more ripping spheres of energy in different cells, and right after each manifestation, I took four or five pictures. On each occasion, only one picture showed an orb reflecting the camera flash as it flitted through the room. My experimental procedures supported my hypothesis that these energy signatures indicated the appearance of an orb, and none of the other 60 or more pictures I took showed signs of anything out of the ordinary. The fact that I couldn't explain why these wavy energy occurrences were happening didn't bother me as much as I had expected it would. This may have been the first time that I let the "What" become more important to me than the "Why" of the events I encountered. I wanted to see more orbs and, in doing so, to work on expanding my "validation" procedures!

Much like the appearance of my friend and Spirit Guide, the Panther, during my Reiki training, it took another series of unanticipated events to overwhelm my disbelief and set me on the path to accepting my spirit contact efforts. Another interesting situation that helped me along my way is that I have had some success in guiding other people and helping them to interact with metaphysical energy. I thought it might be a one-time event when I was able to direct my family to position themselves in specific spots near a Sedona vortex in order to feel the energy. However, when I found a new haunted location to explore, I helped two complete strangers I met during my tour to have an afternoon of paranormal experiences that they will not soon forget. Then again, it may be that I have been able to "convince" spirits to interact with the people around me, but the result was the same: I became a "medium."

Burlington County Prison, in Mount Holly, New Jersey, is a small facility with only three floors. It is a nice museum, with many displays commemorating the prisoners and staff that were there, and the building has been kept in great shape. It is also one of the more paranormally "active" places I have toured. Upon a recommendation from my friend who suggested the Eastern State Penitentiary tour, I scheduled a trip to check out this Mount Holly landmark. I would like to say I planned the trip thoroughly, but the truth is that the only things I knew about the prison were the address and the directions to get there. When I parked in the lot, I realized that the building itself was not very large at all, and there was a rear courtyard. A walkthrough would take a total of 30 minutes, tops, so I felt a little disappointed, since it took over an hour to get there. I was even more disappointed when the building was not open; it is a County-managed museum, but no one showed up to open it at the proper time. When the museum attendant finally unlocked the front door 40 minutes late, he let me in for no charge. I told him I was there for my own paranormal investigation, and he stated he was a skeptic who wanted his own visual proof before he believed the place was haunted.

Yet then he proceeded to describe this one event in his parents' home that he couldn't explain. A family member had passed away, and the family was in mourning. About a week after the funeral, something had compelled him to stand in the middle of the living room and call out to the house. Unbidden, I saw a vision appear about three feet in front of his face of a framed, color picture showing a man around age 30. The man looked like the attendant, but with some differences with his hair style and chin shape. In the vision, this portrait was hanging on a wall, near the bottom of a staircase leading up to the second floor of the building. As the "movie" advanced, the portrait of the young man vibrated on the wall without falling off its hook. When I saw this rattling in the vision, I stepped back in surprise, and the attendant stopped his story to ask me why I had reacted that way. I told him to keep going, and I would reveal the reason for my reaction soon. His story was that he called out to the family member for some reason he couldn't explain, saying that the family was ok and that he should go rest in peace. I quickly interrupted him to tell him what I had seen:

"And the person's portrait on the 1st floor of your parents' house, near the stairs, rattled on the wall, right?

"Yes, it was strange...I can't explain what I even...wait! How did YOU know that?!"

"Because I just saw it in a vision..."

He was silent for a few moments, and then he shook his head and looked at me a little differently. He was looking out the window in thought when I let him know I was going to head into the prison. I started my self-guided tour on the western wing of the ground floor. The entrance and gift shop are on the main floor, and there is a floor above and a basement below. I walked down the hall to look at the dioramas in cells that showed prisoners on bunk beds and fireplaces for heating. Looking back at the entrance, I saw two young women, one with dark hair and the other blond, enter the prison and talk to the attendant, saying they were creating a video report for their Social Studies class in school. They were talking and laughing loudly as they walked around. I was a bit frustrated that their voices were echoing through the small building, impacting the audio evidence I was collecting during my investigation.

To move away from this audio contamination, I proceeded up the stairs to a landing that led to the warden's house next door to the prison. This hallway was well-lit by the sunlight coming through multiple windows. Through the windows, I could see the old wooden gallows in the rear courtyard as I looked outside, but suddenly I felt what seemed to be a soft feather or strip of cloth touch the top of my forehead, at the base of my hairline. I couldn't be sure of what this was, so I looked at the ceiling and the air around me for cobwebs or fabric hanging down, but the hallway was completely free of both. I walked around the hallway, taking pictures, and turned around to return to the prison stairs. In the same spot in the hallway, I felt another stroke on my forehead, more forceful, more noticeable, and this time, it felt like a wide, sticky cobweb. I still couldn't find any explanation for this contact, so I asked out loud if someone was trying to get my attention. I didn't hear a response, so I finally moved up to the second floor.

I walked slowly in and out of some of the cells, and then I entered a cell used as a debtors' prison, with several preserved murals drawn by previous inhabitants of the cell. After looking at the murals, I moved into the far left corner of the cell to face the alcove on the opposite wall. When I reached the left corner, I walked in a space that felt like it was full of sticky strands that clung to my skin, yet there was nothing there! I still couldn't see anything that might cause this, but I felt like I had walked into three thick cobweb strands, one diagonally across my face and one sticking to each of my forearms. The immediate area seemed to be much colder, even with the afternoon sun warming the cell through a window. This was incredible! The sticky web sensations lasted at least 15 seconds. When I walked over into the alcove across the room, the cold spot followed me into the alcove and then dissipated. I tried to experience the cold spot and cobwebs again, but to no avail. Was this ectoplasmic contact from a roaming entity?

As I was leaving the cell, I heard the two young ladies cry out, surprised because they didn't expect a statue to be in one of the cells. I rolled my eyes and walked down the hall to politely ask them to keep their voices down, but they walked right up to me and asked me if I would mind being interviewed for their school report on the history - and the paranormal experiences - of the prison. I asked them how their Social Studies teacher would react to their report including a paranormal element, but they wanted the report to cover both topics, since the history could help explain the hauntings. Then they asked me if I thought the prison was haunted. I told them that I was certain that it was, but I stopped before I described what I had just experienced in the debtor's cell. Something tugged at my sensitivity, and I decided to follow an unexpected thought: why not have each of THEM stand in the same corner and see if they experience anything? In my mind, I sent out the thought that I would like whoever connected with me to make themselves known to these girls as well, yet I received no noticeable response. I asked the dark-haired girl to give the video camera to her friend and walk into that far left corner, with no hint about why. She walked right in and stood in the spot: "Why am I standing here....ewwww! What IS that?! It's sticky and cold on my arms and neck!" Her friend couldn't believe what was happening, so I asked her to stand in that spot as well. At first, the blond said she felt nothing, but then, "Oh my God - what is that on my leg?! It's like a spider web!" And then the paranormal tour really began.

The three of us moved down the hall, still talking about the amazing cobweb experiences. The Dungeon, the name used for the Death Row cell in the center of the top floor, was closed and locked, so we couldn't go inside. The next cell was an open room full of artifacts and memorabilia, including a hangman's hood and a noose. We entered and walked around, and immediately, we started feeling the ectoplasmic strands touching our faces, arms, and legs. The cold, static-filled filament I felt was making contact with me for 3-4 seconds at a time; the electrically charged cobwebs left lasting static on me, making the hair on my arms and legs stand up. The room was very active, and the young women were excited and a little fearful of the intensity of the activity. At one point, one of the girls cried out in surprise when she felt these strands wrap around both of her legs at the same time, and we never found a physical source that explained these phenomena. For over 30 minutes, we walked around the small room, continuing to be touched by unseen sticky strands, while I silently reached out to the entity in the room to ask for the interactions to go on. I didn't feel any indication that I received a response, but the ectoplasmic activity and cold spots trailed us throughout the room. When we walked out of the cell, the girls asked me to give them some additional testimonial statements for their report. I stood against one wall and started to answer their questions as they recorded my comments. Every few minutes, however, "someone" kept stroking the back of my neck at the hairline, but we didn't capture any visual evidence of it. Then they interviewed each other, and God help me if they presented their testimonial to their class:

"Well, when we first got into the prison, there was nothing going on. We walked around and didn't see anything. Then, we met this older guy, and he took us to all these dark cells. Suddenly, there was all this touching! We got touched all over, and it was creepy, but we liked it!"

My response: "No, no, no, NOOOO! PLEASE do not put *THAT* in your video report! Your teacher is gonna call the police to arrest me!"

After we finished laughing, we continued on our joint tour. The fair-haired young woman asked on the way down the second-floor hall if I believed in ghosts. I thought it was kind of an odd question, since we had all experienced paranormal ectoplasm several times already, but an insight came to me: she wasn't really asking me; she was asking herself. I turned the question around and asked her if she believed, and she responded, "I think so." She went on to describe some strange occurrences in her family's home, in which personal objects of hers, like hair brushes and perfume bottles, would disappear from where she left them and then turn up in a completely different room. She was adamant that she did not misplace these objects herself. As she named some of the other objects, another vision came to me, overlaying her face like a movie. I saw another portrait with an old frame hanging on a wall in a house. This picture, however, was in black and white. It was of a distinguished-looking man in his mid-forties, and he was dressed as if he were from the 1940s or 1950s. He had slicked-down hair and a broad mustache. When the young woman saw my expression change, she asked me what was wrong. I decided not to fully describe the portrait, so I asked her if she had a black-and-white portrait of an older man hanging on the wall. She confirmed this, and then I went on to describe the hair, eyes, and mustache, and she stared back at me, speechless. She told me that it was her grandfather. I asked her if she had known him well, thinking the answer would be "yes," but the portrait in my vision flashed once, and the intuitive messages associated with the vision informed me that this was a "no" indicator. She confirmed that she had never actually met him, and then the vision portrait flashed twice and rattled on the wall of her house. I looked at her and chuckled slyly. She looked at me suspiciously and asked, "Whaaaaat?" My response was, "Welllll, that may change sooner than you think. Just remember that I was the one who told you..." She and her friend said they were both getting goosebumps after my answer, and we moved on with the tour.

In Burlington County Prison that day, I experienced the amazing ectoplasmic cobweb feeling twelve different times in three hours. After the girls left, I performed some experiments to see if anyone else felt this webbing in the cells. Other tourists would enter the chamber of artifacts, look around the room, and then walk out of the chamber. They never sensed or felt a thing. I immediately walked through the doorway they had just exited, and I walked into an extensive "column" of thick ectoplasmic strands that covered my face and neck. (I have returned to Burlington County Prison at least four times so far, and I have had some type of experience every time. With its history and displays, I highly recommend a visit even if you aren't interested in having a paranormal encounter.)

All in all, my first of many visits to this prison was amazing. When I reflected upon the visions, interactions, and observed phenomena later, I felt like my sensitivity was at a heightened level, especially when my intuitive connection to that entity was strong enough to encourage it to interact with other people. I certainly don't believe I compelled the entity to do anything at all, but my intuitive feedback indicated that we did communicate at some level. This visit was inspirational to me; it was time to accept that my sensitivity had evolved beyond Reiki energy healing. I couldn't "hide" behind the Reiki excuse for what I was experiencing, and it was scary and liberating at the same time. I knew that the Declaration about my sensitivity was true; that doesn't mean I accepted it and integrated it into my self-definition.

The mortuary in Tombstone was not done with me, either; it held more insights to assist in my acceptance that I was on the right path. During one visit, I received a message that I didn't know how to interpret until a few months later. An entire room of witnesses shared the incredible event with me, even though some of the witnesses had different interpretations of how to explain it. The event took place during the later tour one Friday night. The tour group consisted of two guests, three members of my family, and the Sister Paranormal Investigation team. The SPI sisters ran the tour as they always do, with an introduction to the building and an extended lights-out session with meters and other equipment in use. The activity was pretty frequent during the beginning of the tour, but then things seemed to go a bit quiet. I tried to help get more responses by asking new questions and encouraging more interaction with the group. My seat was facing the front of the building as we sat around the central table, but that didn't stop me from seeing the event. Over my left shoulder, I saw an extended flash of light that lit up half of the front room with a dim, white pulse. Although I could not hear it, I felt the sensation of a concussive force wash over me, like a silent thunderclap, accompanying the pulse of light. The guests were facing that direction and said the light seemed to come from beyond the bar, near the doorway leading to the rear sections of the mortuary. We looked around for a few moments, but we couldn't find the source of the light. The sisters resumed their attempts at communicating with the local spirit population, and the exploding light happened again. I could feel the heaviness of the air after the silent shockwave rippled through the room a second time. Everyone had seen the light pulse, but we still couldn't pinpoint its origin. We turned off the rest of the equipment and unplugged all the light sources we could find. Five minutes later, the amazing light pulse happened a third time.

After the third pulse, Nora announced that she thought this was some sort of Higher Being, like an Angel or a Spirit Guide, trying to contact her. She did mention that it might be my "Polar Panther" as she calls him, but I was certain - don't ask me how - that it was not the Panther. The silent wave of force exploded a fourth time, lighting up two rooms, yet we still couldn't find where it was coming from. This time, I received an intuitive message that this was associated with an entity that resembled a titan from Greek mythology: a heavily-muscled warrior dressed in a white tunic and leather battle kilt, standing with his fists on his hips. With this new overlapping picture in my mind, the light pulse appeared to be coming from the chest of this impressive being with alabaster skin. The exploding ball of force was observed a total of seven times during the two-hour tour, and I even went into the bathroom at the rear of the building to make sure we had some perspective on where the light was coming from. At the end of the evening, we checked our camcorders, but we didn't capture any of these pulses on video. One of the camcorders malfunctioned right before the first pulse emanated from the bar, and the other's battery was almost completely drained, even though it was at full charge at the beginning of the tour. It was an awesome display, and I could feel the incredible power from each light pulse. What did this "visitation" mean? I had no idea. Was I being guided down a new path? Even if I didn't recognize the path, was the path being brought to me? Was it even a path at all? It was a great experience, but I didn't spend a lot of time analyzing it. Maybe I should have. The good news is that I saw these light pulses again in the future, and I immediately recognized them, pulsating from the rope belt of my Spirit Guide monk whom I met during my medium training.

Chapter 9: Mediumship

I couldn't deceive myself anymore. I finally had to concede that I had some level of sensitivity when I decided to begin a new class to learn and practice spiritual communication skills. Just having the desire to pursue training was a clear self-indicator that I was ready to accept this evolving gift. It also meant that I wanted to learn ways to shield myself from and attune myself to those higher frequencies of paranormal energy. With this attunement, I couldn't wait to see how I might invoke interaction with spirits and other entities that wish to communicate with me. Outside of learning various mediumistic meditations and procedures, I privately hoped that there was another epiphany waiting for me during my mediumship training that would help me to continue my sensitivity evolution. But first, I had to find a training class.

At the time, I thought that maybe the pursuit of more training would prepare me better for facing the ramifications of the Declaration, so I contacted the Reiki master who presided over my Reiki attunement. In my email to her, I reminded her of when I attended her Reiki I and II Practitioner classes and described my rather unique Spirit Guide, the Panther. After I described some of my experiences with the vortexes and in the mortuary, I asked her for her opinions on my continuing my Reiki studies to become a master myself or my delving into mediumship instead. Her response surprised me by its details as well as its matter-of-fact tone:

"It all depends on what you want to develop. Most of the mediums here are also energy healers, so it would be a natural step for you to move in this direction. You would, however, need to decide whether it is spirit-rescue mediumship, which is working with uncrossed entities such as the ones you have been dealing with on the ghost tours, or whether you would like to bring through Loved Ones for people.[11]"

My scientific mind was almost in shock: "Am I *really* having this conversation?" She said it would be a natural step for me to move in this direction. *Natural*? Natural for WHOM?! In what world is this "natural?!" I could tell anyone willing to listen about the details of my Reiki experiences, but it still struck me as odd that she could talk about these metaphysical studies with the same level of calm as if she were giving someone directions to a store. I immediately noticed that there wasn't a single comment in her email in support of my continuing my Reiki studies to become a master. I read her email several times, making sure I didn't miss anything, but I had already decided that my own choice would be to develop my sensitivity into the spirit realm. But how would I start? Unfortunately, her office was no longer hosting the "Mediumship for Beginners" course. I called around to several professed mediums, but I could not find anyone who was teaching classes at that time. However, I had convinced myself that I needed to take a class, learning new theories and techniques to practice. Rather than wait up to a year or more for a class to begin somewhere, I decided, right or wrong, to give an online class a try. The entire curriculum's material was available online, and there were videos of taped classes to help with explaining and demonstrating techniques. I am still working through this online class right now, moving in and out of the training as time permits. Yet the practical application of what I have learned so far has taken off.

The online mediumship course is organized according to levels of progressive development, instructing the student on how to master and protect his own energy before trying to invite spiritual contact. The initial chapters of the mediumship book are written to prepare the student for his first interaction with a spirit entity, and I learned some techniques for basic meditation and for grounding my energy, with some theories being similar to those of Reiki. I practiced shielding myself with both golden and white shields for different protective purposes. I engaged in energy running, drawing white energy from the God Source and green energy from the Earth in alternate waves. I stripped away negative energy from my base energy by projecting it through a metaphysical sieve to strain away the unwanted debris and cleanse myself. (This sure sounds like acceptance, doesn't it?) I cannot deny that I was a little skeptical about these exercises; my original thought was a person needed to have some innate medium abilities first before they could perform these exercises. However, my Reiki training and the idea that anyone can *intend* to heal another with energy helped me keep an open mind about learning parallel methodologies for spirit medium work.

What I find interesting is that the first experience I had in the training was during an energy cleansing exercise, when I tried to project my energy through a mental sieve to cleanse it. I envisioned this glimmering silver mesh wall in front of me, and I sent my personal energy forward to be strained through the mesh. Sending my energy through this strainer was supposed to help filter out negative material from my energy field. I was confused, though, when I felt a few of the thin wires of the mesh get snagged in several places on my aura; this energy sieve was actually removing negative "debris." Next, I envisioned another wall of a much finer mesh, and this time, I felt like I was straining my chest and head through this wall, again with charcoal-colored negativity being left behind on the mesh. It was a strange feeling, like I had just stripped away a layer of doubt so that I could feel more calmness. I was so surprised by the filtering sensation that I exited out of my meditative state and commented out loud, "Well THAT was weird..." That sensation helped me to understand that intention and direction were also components of my mediumistic activities. Once again, a metaphysical experience outside of my expectations inspired me to dig deeper into this new medium field.

There were several "signs" that encouraged me to accelerate my medium studies. Once I started sensing these different levels of energy,

I wanted to make sure I was able to control the various spirit interactions I was initiating, and more importantly, protect myself from any unwanted intrusions. It was a critical step for my acceptance of these experiences to make sure I was comfortable with my ability to shield myself. I did recognize the strength of my personal shield during my exposure to the Sedona vortexes, so I had some level of confidence. What I hadn't considered is that there may be entities or energies trying to contact me because THEY want to on their own. This actually happened to me while I was in the office late one Friday night. On this evening, I had to finish some work, but I ended up spending over two hours talking with a friend about many of my crazy Reiki experiences over the past few months. When the two of us left his office, he walked with me to the elevators on my way out of the building. We were on the third floor, looking through the interior walls of glass into the building's atrium. While I was waiting for the elevator, my friend mentioned that one of the elevators on the other side of the building appeared to go up and down between floors late at night. The doors would open for a few moments and then close, and then the elevator would move to the next floor. Perhaps it was a safety feature to ensure at least one elevator was working. The elevators were glass on the outside, so I could easily see if anyone was inside. Although I was only slightly interested in this activity, I casually gazed across the atrium to the elevators on the other side. Sure enough, the left elevator was moving up from the 1st floor to the 2nd floor, and the car itself was empty. I watched it stop at the 2nd floor, its doors opening on their own. After a few seconds, the doors started to close, so it seemed to be pretty standard, and then I saw a dark shadow figure enter the elevator car! It appeared almost two-dimensional, but I could see how it turned its "body" to the left to dart through the closing doors. When it was inside, it squared its shoulders, and it looked out into the atrium. Its gaze traveled up to the 3rd floor, and it locked eyes with me! At that moment, I received an extra-sensory intuition that this was some type of visitation. Even now, I don't know what the message of the visitation was; perhaps the visit WAS the message. The shadow figure lingered for only a few seconds and then disappeared. My friend watched my jaw drop, and, in light of our two-hour conversation, he said, "DON'T tell me you just saw something! Don't TELL me that! I have to go back and work for several more hours!" This experience gave me something new to consider; I needed to begin incorporating steps like shielding and grounding into my daily regimen of activities if I wanted to continue to delve into my mediumistic abilities. You can never predict when someone wants to talk to you...

Another component of the course teaches techniques for effective meditation. For as restful as it can be, meditation is not necessarily easy for everyone. My practice attempts at entering a deep meditation were challenging not because I couldn't clear my mind but because I kept falling asleep! I would sink down into a trance-like state, but I had trouble maintaining it without drifting away into a soothing nap. My mind was sufficiently alert to force myself awake, which helped with preparing for the next attempt, but that wasn't enough. When I couldn't figure out how to maintain an extended meditative state, I read about how this was a common question for people new to meditation. A clever idea was to create a different mental stimulus for the subconscious mind to focus on. One recommendation was to balance a glass of water on my leg, with the intention that my subconscious mind would stay alert enough to prevent me from falling asleep and spilling the water down my thigh. It seemed like a good idea, so I gave it a try. After grabbing a towel and drying off my jeans, I had to come up with a new option. I sunk down into another meditation and reached out with my senses to detect any energy or frequency fluctuation that might come to me. Ironically, I had just found the key to my meditative state: my mental focus on energy distortions kept my mind occupied enough for me to stay awake.

My successful cleansing, "running," and meditation exercises gave me the confidence to try my first intentional spiritual contact. The exercises included creating a mental "waiting room," complete with personalized decorations and two comfy chairs. Within my meditative state, I was supposed to walk to the door and enter the room. The mental process was to envision myself sitting in one of the plush chairs and to invite someone to take the seat next to me, with the idea of asking him or her a few questions that would help solidify the connection. First, I had to choose a Loved One to invite into my special waiting room. I had been prepared to meet with my maternal grandmother, as I came up with several unanswered questions for her about our family and her life. However, when I settled into my calm mental state, something made me change my mind; I selected my maternal grandfather instead. Maybe it was because I had always thought of him as a staunch supporter of my family, or maybe it was because some members of my extended family never had a chance to meet him before he passed away. I have modeled my own relationships with my family after many of the things he did. I drifted into my meditation, envisioned myself walking into the room, and sat down in the chair on the right. Without knowing how to address a Loved One in this scenario, I started by inviting him to speak to me by calling out his full legal name, but nothing happened. After a few moments, I called him by the name I used for him all my life: Pop-pop. Still nothing. I was going to give up, but then I witnessed another door in the room glide open, a door that I hadn't put there myself. The image of my grandfather, at an age a few years before he passed, stood in the doorway. He smiled, and the next thing I knew, I saw his back and rear as he was sitting down in the empty chair. I never saw him cross the room to the chair, which was a little disconcerting, but at that point, I was more concerned with the fact that I hadn't come up with a good question to ask him. I kept going over what he might be thinking or doing "now," but I finally asked myself, "Well, what would HE want to talk about?" As soon as I projected this thought into my waiting room, I felt a wave of warmth wash over my left shoulder, and I heard my grandfather's distinctive voice in my mind, saying, "You mean how proud I am of you?" This was a completely unexpected response, so much so that I was jolted out of my meditation when my attention moved to the distracting smile that developed on my face. I chuckled out loud when I remembered the thought and the sensation of his energy. The thought of him praising me never entered my conscious mind at all; I was so focused on trying to guess his thoughts that this totally surprised me. Maybe there was something to this mediumship thing after all...

Another surprising exercise was geared toward sending out an invitation to meet my Spirit Guide. The Panther was very clear that he would not be able to assist me with my paranormal pursuits, but he didn't answer one way or the other when I asked how I should proceed; he simply said, "I will always be with you." Now that I had formed my waiting room, I was able to use this mental space again to invite my Spirit Guide to come sit with me. This time, I was determined to have a wizard for a Guide, and I imagined this light gray robed man with a staff and a gnarled beard coming to sit with me...and once again, I failed to force my Spirit Guide into the wizard form that I wanted. I told myself I was "supposed" to have a wizened sorcerer as a Spirit Guide for medium work, since I had attempted to "make" one to serve as my Reiki Spirit Guide and had failed. I really don't know why I was so "certain" that I would have a Spirit Guide who looked like a wizard, yet I tried anyway. (Obviously, I was showing how much I knew about Spirit Guides - next to nothing.) I gave up on coercing my Spirit Guide into the empty chair of my mental room. I sent my thoughts into the room that I hoped to meet my Guide soon, and then I "heard" a creak of wood, and standing over me was a tall figure in a charcoal-gray, homespun robe. Pale hands stuck out of threadbare seams on the arms of the robes, but when I looked up at the figure's face, the hood of the robe was full of swirling gray smoke. To this day, I haven't yet seen my Spirit Guide's face, but when I met him, I received ESP messages that this was a monk. The most striking aspect of the unnamed monk was the rope belt around his waist. The pristine white rope was so bright that it seemed incandescent. When I focused on it, I saw this rope pulse with white light. After a few moments, the rope pulsed again, radiating a dim white light that filled the entire waiting room in my meditation. The rope belt flashed three more times, and I received intuitive messages that I had seen this repeating light pulse before. It took me a few moments to remember that it was the same intensity and frequency as the exploding flashes of concussive force I experienced few weeks earlier in the Watt & Tarbell mortuary! Nora did say that she sensed the light pulses were due to a Spirit Guide or another Higher Being, but she said it was coming to meet her. Was this actually my monk making himself known back in Tombstone? The monk has not confirmed or denied it, but the extra-sensory messages I received when I met him gave me the impression that there was a direct correlation between the phenomena. I guess it really doesn't matter, though; the monk is with me now. After my meditation, I was watching a TV show relating a historical account of missionary activities in the western United States, when the impulse to ask the monk's name came over me. I was half-joking when I started coming up with old names, but when I laughed and said, "Yeah, I bet it's something like Ezekiel," I saw a vision of the incandescent rope belt pulsing. Ezekiel? Really?? It almost sounds *too* contrived, but Ezekiel, it is! Later in the TV program, there was a segment upon Jesuit monks who had hung themselves, and the flashing rope vision returned. Ezekiel mentally impressed upon me that he had not hung himself, but now I knew that my mediumistic Spirit Guide was a Jesuit monk who lived at the end of the 1800s.

The meditation exercises reinforced the processes of grounding and shielding in preparation for contact. The next exercises were designed to hone my spirit sensitivity. One of the exercises directed me to request any spirit looking to communicate with me to enter my field of perception. I was deep in a meditation, and I was waiting for some type of "visual" indication of an energy source. I didn't really see anything in my mental space, but I figured that I can't control when a spirit chooses to communicate. After several attempts, I started to develop a dizzy feeling with some eye discomfort, so I figured I was getting tired. I opted to explore another chapter in the mediumship course rather than try again. I was a little disappointed that I didn't make contact, but I wasn't in a rush. I was comfortable that things would unfold in time. (Of course, they had already begun to unfold...)

A few weeks later, I went back to Burlington County Prison to see if I could repeat the crazy experiences I had. I was looking forward to the ectoplasmic contact I had so many times on my last visit. This time, the prison seemed relatively quiet. I made a beeline for the upstairs artifacts room where there had been so much activity. I wandered around in the chamber for at least 15 minutes, but I didn't feel any of those sticky web sensations. In fact, I felt a little tired, and I wondered if I was coming down with a cold or something, as I felt slightly dizzy and was developing a headache. Wait a minute: a headache with dizziness in this chamber, and ONLY in this chamber, over the course of the entire trip? Maybe this is an indicator for me that I am sensing paranormal energy! I asked out loud for someone to show me a sign that I wasn't alone in this room, and I felt a pinpoint pain behind my left eye along with this dizzy disorientation. A few minutes later, some unseen force touched my elbow and stroked the back of my neck. Then the dizzy feeling went away, and I did not feel the eye pain anymore. Could this mean that the energy had dissipated? I continued my self-guided tour for another hour without much to show for it. I might have experienced a cold spot in the old shower room, but I had no way of verifying it. In the basement level, I wandered through the kitchen, the workshop, and the remaining cells without detecting any activity, but when I looked into the utility room, I observed an energy distortion of rippling lines and immediately snapped several pictures. The first picture out of five showed a spherical orb behind the table in the room; the other pictures showed nothing. While examining the digital photos, something touched my shoulder; I spun around, but there was nothing there. The activity of the tour wasn't quite as distinctive as it was on my previous tour, but I was still satisfied with the experiences I did have. More importantly, I had uncovered what I thought to be a new level of sensitivity that created a physical reaction in me, affecting my body's equilibrium. I had to find more ways to test this theory.

The remarkable activity we had during our ghost tour at Watt & Tarbell's mortuary in Tombstone held amazing potential for experimenting with my sensitivity if we could encourage the "residents" to interact with us again. Evidence for the documentary about the history and haunting of the mortuary was still being collected as well, so I planned another trip to my paranormal "home away from home" to see my new friends and capture more material. My family joined me, and we arrived in the middle of the afternoon. The founders of Sister Paranormal Investigators, Nora and Stacy, were outside, talking with visitors and encouraging them to join one of the evening tours. I went inside and sat down on one of the theater benches to talk with Nora about the experiences I had at the Burlington County Prison. As soon as I sat down, I felt the air around me become thick and heavy. Very quickly, I had a sensation of dizziness, and the room started to spin. A sharp pain behind my right eye caused me to clamp my eyes shut. Nora looked at me and laughed, "Ha-ha, now they are saying 'Hello' to you, and they are leaving me alone! I'm gonna head to the back room." And she left me alone with "them!" It was exciting but a little frustrating; if "they" were saying "hello" to me, why couldn't I make out any voices or other extra-sensory perceptions? The intensity of my disorientation continued to increase, and I finally stood up shakily and walked to the door. As soon as I stepped outside of the building, the dizziness faded away, and the piercing eye pain disappeared. I walked around the streets of Tombstone for a while to test my theory that this equilibrium shift was some kind of paranormal energy sensitivity, rather than just a coincidental discomfort, and I didn't have any of the symptoms again on my walk...until I entered the building once more. I asked the mortuary's "residents" to leave me alone for the time being, promising to try and communicate with them later, and the disorientation went away. I didn't feel any of these symptoms for the rest of my visit, but we had another evening of amazing ghost experiences.

There is no other way to describe it: the Watt & Tarbell mortuary is a hotbed of paranormal activity. I have visited it many times, and the spirit experiences and interactions appeal to both the analytical and metaphysical portions of my mind. Even on what the sisters called a "slow night," the ghost tour I joined still experienced many different phenomena, like hearing disembodied voices with our own ears and calling out to unseen entities and hearing their responses through the spirit box. I have been touched by chilling fingers, felt icy breath on my cheek for several minutes, seen floating light anomalies with my own eyes, and even seen shadow figures moving in well-lit areas. Along with these experiences, I have captured many audio and video clips that document the paranormal activity of strobing light orbs, electronic voice phenomena undetected by my ears, and other intelligent interactions with the guests on the tours. It has not ceased to fascinate me, and I've come to the realization that it continues to help me in the evolution of my sensitivity. It was also the place where I had my first mediumistic experience with actual spirit communication that I could understand.

On a more recent trip to Tombstone, I brought several of my family members to visit our "extended family" and see how the sisters' new store was doing. They rented the building next door to expand their business, and people had reported activity in the new building as well. I had decided to bring my new family member, a four-month-old puppy, with us as a socialization exercise for the puppy to get more comfortable around strangers. I was sitting on a bench outside of the store, just watching the tourists go by and letting them greet and pet my adorable but shy puppy, when my first spiritual contact of the day took place. Someone was asking me what kind of breed the puppy was when the street around me started to spin. I felt very dizzy, and the pinpoint stabbing of pain shot through my left eye. I tried to shake off the discomfort, but it wasn't until I asked whoever was trying to communicate with me to wait until later that the pain finally vanished. An hour later, I walked through the sitting area of the store, and a wave of dizziness came over me, but on this occasion, I was overcome with chills due to this cold spot on my shoulder. I was confused about my next steps, and I finally remembered my medium training. It took me until this trip, months after I had met my mediumship Spirit Guide, Ezekiel, to actually ask him for help with the communication attempts in the mortuary. (Unlike the Panther, Ezekiel didn't tease me or pretend to be exasperated by how long it took me to think of asking for his help. He nodded once, touched the white shield that I maintain around me, and walked away from me, disappearing after a few steps. In response, the Panther just said, "I had to break you, so his job is a lot easier...he should thank me." I'm not sure when he started comparing me to a wild horse to be tamed...)

The ghost tour that evening was more quiet than usual in terms of the spirit-box communication. There were some responses, but they were less frequent than on previous tours. One significant name that did come through very clearly was "Cochise," and it had never been heard within the mortuary before. Later that evening, several of the guests, including myself, heard a disembodied voice with our own ears that sounded like a Native American chant or war cry coming from behind the bar. However, Nora suggested that "somebody like Jeff should go up by the bar" for a portion of the investigation, so that I could try stirring up more interaction with the spirits. (Isn't it nice when your friends offer you up as an experimental guinea pig or a "sacrifice?") Well, it worked. The sisters had set up a laser light grid on me, so that the audience could see if there was a shift or even a blocking out of one or more of the dots of light on the grid. I started out by asking for Indian Charlie to come join me at the bar. Multiple people watched a light anomaly come out of the corner near me, float toward me, make contact with my outstretched forearm, and float away. There was also a separate floating light orb that flew out from behind the back of my neck and down my arm, and I asked, "Is there someone touching my neck right now?" because I felt that physical contact. Other people saw shadow figures walk behind me, and a few saw my shirt get tugged, distorting the laser light grid on my sleeve. Most of these phenomena were captured in a night-vision video to record evidence of the encounters, but during the tour, I didn't experience the energy equilibrium disruption or dizziness that signals mediumistic communication. That happened after the tour.

With all of my high-tech video and audio equipment, I also brought a simple pair of dowsing rods with me. My dowsing rods are thin copper bars, each bent in the shape of an "L" with the shorter end sitting inside of a separate copper tube that serves as a handle. The handle allows the rod to rotate freely in a 360-degree circle. Dowsing techniques have been used to search for underground water, metals and gems, and even human gravesites. Using the theory that paranormal events can introduce electromagnetic energy, these copper conductors can get magnetized when energy is traveling down them due to contact with an entity, allowing them to attach to each other with a weak magnetic force. Spirits can also move them and make them spin, so they can be used in question-and-answer sessions as pointers.

In the hands of Nora, the rods were really impressive. Standing in the bar area, she asked the spirit residents to rotate the rods and point to people or locations that answered her questions. She would ask that the rods point to "her biological sister," and the copper rods slowly rotated about 90 degrees from their original position, and both finally halted when they were pointing at Stacy. When this started, however, I began receiving sensations, twinges at the edges of my sensitivity that indicate someone was trying to communicate with me, as the room started to spin. I was so disoriented that I had to sit down in the next room and put my head between my legs to fight the nausea and pain. I couldn't hear all of Nora's next question, but I later found out that she asked the entity holding the rods to point her "confidant." All of the witnesses told me that the rods quickly rotated and pointed toward me while I was sitting in the other room. I didn't hear her question because I was focusing on probing around me with my sensitivity. I intuitively knew that some entity was trying to impart a message to me, but I wasn't "listening" the right way, or else I didn't know how to translate the message into something I could understand. The increasing dizziness and nausea didn't help at all, and I finally asked whoever was attempting to communicate with me to try something different. (Think of it like talking to someone who doesn't speak English; the person won't suddenly understand you if you speak louder, so you have to try something else.) Later, I realized that I hadn't really tried other ways to interpret the messages myself, but in the moment, the dizziness and discomfort drove me to say out loud in desperation, "C'mon! This isn't working! I really want to know what you want to say to me, but you gotta try something else!" Immediately, I felt the dizziness subside, but the disorientation didn't go away completely. During this same time frame, Nora had asked if it was Indian Charlie was moving the rods. I heard her ask the question, but as if in response to her, I received two different names as thoughts in my head at the same time: Adam and Peter. Both are entities who have commonly talked with visitors on the tours in the past, so I recognized the names. However, I didn't understand how I was supposed to interpret BOTH names coming to my mind at the same time. Mentally, I asked that they give me a clearer answer on who was moving the rods right then. Suddenly, a brief vision of a piece of parchment appeared in my mind, and upper-case block letters started to appear on the parchment, spelling out "A...D...A...M" with no writing implement being shown. The letters appeared one at a time, with about a half-second in between letters. As Nora finished her question about Indian Charlie and waited, I interjected in a distant, off-handed tone, "No, it's Adam." Nora asked for confirmation of Adam's presence, and the two rods spun not once but three times in a full circle! With this confirmation, the group started asking questions of Adam to test his abilities. When Nora asked if Indian Charlie was near her, I immediately answered in a soft voice, "No...he is standing in that corner." I felt some mental "pull" to that area just when she asked the question. (Incidentally, this was the same corner where the floating ball of light that touched my arm came from. The other light anomaly that shot from behind my neck also went toward that corner.) To the guests' amazement, the two rods rotated almost 180 degrees to point into the corner that I had indicated.

Later in the dowsing rod session, the two rods were spinning at different speeds and in opposite directions, and my extra-sensory intuition informed me that Peter had "grabbed" the rod in Nora's right hand, so Adam and Peter were manipulating them separately. When the line of questioning asked the different entities to move one rod at a time, one rod would point to the person who was the answer to the question, and the other rod would point straight ahead without moving. With all of the tour guests asking different, unscripted questions, it was an incredible series of answers. When the left rod would be moving slowly or would stop altogether, I sensed that I could communicate with Adam verbally, encouraging him to expend more energy and move the rods faster: "C'mon, Adam! You can do this! Put your back into it! You can do better than that! THERE ya go! Thank you, Adam!" After the dowsing rod session, my family and the sisters were looking at me in wonder, and I just shrugged my shoulders. I privately thanked my Spirit Guide, Ezekiel, for helping me to make contact with Adam, Peter, and Indian Charlie, and we finished the night's investigations in the tunnels beneath the mortuary. (On another note, the bottom stair leading down to the tunnels had a strange heat signature on the outer face of the step that I captured with my thermal imager. Even with my many attempts to replicate it manually, I still can't explain why there was a hot spot there or why it lasted so long when others from human handprints, shoes, and legs faded away before it did...)

In the weeks to come, I continued to test my sensitivity in reportedly haunted locations. The dizziness and disorientation is a small price to pay if I am exposed to more opportunities to experiment with my spirit communication ability. I planned these trips to experience the energy disorientation and see what I can do with it. At this point, I am not yet comfortable with attempting to "summon" entities to me, so I have no choice but to travel to the entities' haunts to interact with spirit energy. (I really need to get back into my mediumship course; I am guessing it will save me some money...) The travel was worth it when I felt those paranormal energy "twinges" that pulled at the edges of my sensitivity, indicating the manifestation of some type of entity, and it started to happen more frequently as I practiced. As an example, my sister-in-law and I decided to take a ghost tour just before Halloween at the Merchants' House in New York City[12]. The Tredwell family lived in the house for almost 100 years, and they left behind the only intact family home from the 1900s in New York City, complete with furnishings, decorations, and some personal items. Paranormal activity has been reported there for many years, and I had never been to the museum, so I was looking forward to testing my sensitivity there. The two of us were standing outside on the street, waiting for the museum doors to open, while we were talking about the variety of equipment I had brought with me for the tour. I asked her if she wanted to use the equipment with me or just wander through the house to see if she experienced anything. While she was answering, I felt a pinpoint prick behind my right eye, and I sensed some type of energy disturbance of a strange frequency. She watched as I looked off into the distance and then slowly turned toward the building. My attention was drawn upward and to the right, and my gaze finally rested on the middle window of the third floor, where I saw a rippling energy distortion *inside* the window. When she asked me what I saw, I merely said, "There is something going on in that room."

The doors to the museum opened, and I had to face the frustration that they would not allow digital cameras, video camcorders, or audio recorders in the museum. Photography is allowed during the day tours, so this didn't make any sense. Grudgingly, I turned in my backpack full of equipment, and we started the tour. We traveled up two flights of stairs to enter the first bedroom. As the docent talked about the Tredwell family member who lived in this room, she played recordings of people describing the paranormal activity they had experienced in this bedroom. But I wasn't paying attention. I felt a little dizziness and turned around to face a closet behind me; my sensitivity was being "pulled" toward this door. My sister-in-law turned to ask me a question, but she saw me facing the closet door. After a moment, I told her, "Just wait until we go into the next room. Something is happening in there..." What I didn't know was this was a shared closet between two bedrooms, so the tour proceeded through this closet door to the second bedroom. I was standing in the far right corner of the room, and I could feel a breeze coming through the fireplace vent, so I was becoming skeptical about the "cold spots" the docent was describing. I looked across the dark room to the opposite corner, and I saw a dull gray image appear out of nowhere. I stared at that image for three full seconds; I couldn't believe it - an apparition of an old man's gnarled hand, clenching his fingers into a fist! The hand floated from the left window and into the wall next to it. I stood there speechless, tugging on my sister-in-law's sweater to get her attention. When the docent finished her stories, I tried to ask the tour group if anyone else had seen this apparition, but the docent interrupted my question: "Please, sir - save ALL questions until the end of the tour. My colleague is waiting to take you to the next room, so please follow her." (Yes, this kind of pissed me off...) Walking to the next room downstairs, I touched my sister-in-law on the shoulder and whispered in a hiss, "I can't believe it...that tour guide just snapped at me, and I was trying to ask everyone if they saw that apparition of a floating hand closing its fingers into a fist!" She hadn't seen anything herself, but she was excited for me. Her next thought brought her up short; she stopped in her tracks and turned to face me as we both whispered intently:

Sister-in-law: "You DO realize that that was the window you pointed out while we were waiting outside, don't you? Where you said you saw something?"

Me: "What? Wow, I forgot all about that...no, that's not it; that was up on the third floor in the middle of the building..."

Sister-in-law (interrupting): "...and this IS the third floor, and that was the middle window. There is another small room on the other side of that wall, and it has a window, too..."

Me: "Are you kidding me?! That's THE window?! No way! NO WAY! I can't believe it!"

The rest of the tour was uneventful, and the air downstairs was calm and normal, unlike the heavy atmosphere upstairs. We finished the tour in the kitchen, and the docent announced, "So, did someone have a question earlier, upstairs in Mr. Tredwell's room?" I raised my hand, and I couldn't help but correct her, telling her that I really wanted a confirmation if anyone had seen the apparition of the man's hand! She was genuinely apologetic after she heard my account, and I described the apparition of the wrinkled hand "fanning" its fingers closed one by one to make a fist. We then talked about some of the volunteers' experiences in the museum while we headed for the exit, and several of them were nervous about closing up the museum at night. I turned away from the front door to talk with the docent when I saw a wavy energy distortion on the flight of stairs leading up to the second floor...but the door was closed. I cocked my head to the right as the rippling image remained for a few seconds, and I asked, "What's going on on the stairs?" The guide said it was probably one of the other volunteers cleaning up. After I asked how many volunteers there were in the museum this evening, I realized all of them were accounted for downstairs on the first floor. When I pointed this out, the docent asked me if I wanted to go open the door. "Hell YES, I do!" I walked to the door and slowly pulled it open, stepping out from in front of the doorway so that I would not block out any of the light from the lamps behind me. It took me a second to realize what I was seeing: the light went through the doorway and up to the fourth step, but on the fifth step, there was a large shadow that absorbed the light from going any further up the stairs. The strange part was that the light went *around* this column of shadow on either side, so I could see steps 6, 7, and 8 on the left and right sides of the stairway. After a few more seconds, a wave of cold flew at me from the open doorway and passed through me, as if the shadow form had just made contact with me, and then I could see the entire stairway in the dim light. At that point, the docent reached my side and peered around me to look up the stairs. Before I spoke to her about the shadow, I heard footsteps coming from up the stairs, sounding like two hard heels walking on the first landing. I turned to her to make sure she had heard the footsteps, and she was staring up the stairway when she said, "Yes...yes I did...holy sh___..." It was quite a tour, and I definitely want to return for a daytime museum tour to take pictures and video. (My experiences have been recorded by one of the museum's historians to add to the annals of the paranormal claims in the Merchants' House.)

With all of these events helping me to unlock my sensitivity, I feel like my developing medium skills are just the tip of the iceberg. My intuitions tell me that until I can interpret these attempts at spirit communication, I still have a long way to go. On the other hand, I have come far with identifying my "early warning signs" of paranormal activity. At some point along the way, I noticed that I still had to find answers to a few questions about this journey of spiritual growth. I had accepted my sensitivity, but had I really embraced it? In order to have any hope of unifying the Metaphysical and Engineering portions of my mind, I needed better explanations about what had happened to me that appealed to both of them.

Chapter 10: Enlightenment

As different as the Panther and the Jesuit monk are in terms of their personalities and the manner in which I talk with them, I truly appreciate how they have chosen to guide and direct me in Reiki healing and in spirit mediumship. They have never stepped on each other's toes in providing me direction, and it amazes me how they know not only what to share with me but also how to share it in order to help me along, with their word choice and tone being just as important as the messages they give. As they seem to be serving separate "functions" in my spiritual evolution, I do not believe that I am done with meeting my Spirit Guides. From my studies, I have learned that a person can have anywhere from three to eight Spirit Guides at any given time, and some may help you for specific reasons or during a specific time frame and then move on. There is often a master Guide that directs and oversees the standard Guides, and it is my opinion that I have not yet officially met my master Guide. I don't believe there is a specific reason that has prevented or discouraged this introduction; it just hasn't happened yet. Perhaps it will happen in the future. With everything I have experienced up to this point, I have given up trying to predict what I might learn or see; even when I tried to influence the forms of my Spirit Guides, they demonstrated that I can't control everything. The point is that I am supposed to use my intention and recognize the results. Like the Panther once said to me, "You are the instrument...but I am the Guide."

Their guidance has been inspirational to me in many ways. I have realized that at the critical turning points in my evolution, they have silently agreed that I have to find my own ways to interpret the wisdom that I am supposed to take away from my experiences. They trust me to draw what I need from these events, and they seem to be satisfied with how I have learned those necessary lessons. But there were questions that I had to discover for myself before I could even ask them. As most of us know, learning something on your own and embracing it integrates it into your being and awareness. When you finally accept it, something clicks inside of you, and you realize the truth of the wisdom that you will use going forward. In my case, there was one evening during which several personal truths clicked, and I achieved enlightenment on some of the events related to my spiritual evolution. (As much as it pains me to admit it, the Panther was right: my analytical mind kept getting in the way. The Panther's smug expression on that day made things even worse.) This night of revelation took place, rather appropriately, after a weekend of video interviews and ghost tours in the Watt & Tarbell mortuary in Tombstone, but it happened in my family's home several hundred miles away.

The trip to Tombstone in May was a working one, as I was helping to collect footage for the documentary, but I didn't hesitate to take as many ghost tours as I could. During the day, we were doing interviews with the sisters and having Nora present the audio evidence collected from electronic voice phenomena (EVPs) during recent months. It was about 3pm, and the building's lights were on. I was running a video camcorder focused on the laptop computer with the EVP files sitting on the circular table in the main room, and I was standing in the entryway from the main room to the bar area, facing away from the bar. At one point, I zoomed in to capture the digital sound wave displayed on the screen while listening to a specific voice clip. To my right, just inside the opposite corner of the bar, I saw a column of dark shadow appear out of thin air. This shadow figure appeared as a mass of blackness in the well-lit room, as if all of the light in that corner was being absorbed by the shadow. The shadow image was well within the scope of my visual range, rather than at the peripheral edge of my sight, so I saw the entire figure. The shadow lasted about three seconds before it disappeared. I could see that it was about five and a half feet tall, but I could not make out a specific shape. It was there long enough for me to turn quickly and view it directly an instant before it vanished. As my mind processed what I had just seen, Nora looked up from her laptop and said, "You just saw that, didn't you?" I looked at her and replied, "If you mean that shadow in the corner, then yeah!" We waited a few minutes to see if the shadow would reappear, but it didn't. We resumed the interviews to review the EVPs - and there were some pretty funny and racy EVPs from the "resident" spirits - so that we could review them later in the editing sessions. (This is a "hot" corner in the mortuary, with an original 1881 mortician's table standing against the wall. This is the same corner associated with the other story about the floating light anomalies touching my arm and flying away from my neck.)

About 30 minutes later, we were still capturing raw footage on the EVP reviews. I stepped back from my camcorder to listen to the next EVP, when another shadow manifested in the very same corner of the bar. This time, however, I could make out that the shadow had a head and shoulders! I couldn't tell if it was looking at me, but I saw the human-shaped shadow attempt to move into the room, manifesting a forearm, an elbow, and part of a bicep before vanishing. Nora hit the "Pause" function on the audio software and asked, "You saw that one, too, right?" I described the head and arm movement, as if the shadow figure was trying to step out of the corner and toward the bar. Nora immediately stated that she believed it was Indian Charlie manifesting. I wish we had a camera directed at that corner, because I would love to see if the shadow figure would have been captured. No such luck...

After the interviews, I helped the sisters set up for the first ghost tour of the evening, positioning some testing equipment on the bar: a twist-top flashlight and a mel meter, which reads temperature and electromagnetic fields at the same time. As I was setting up the mel meter, it started going off, its high-pitched beeping detecting a magnetic field nearby. I spun around to look for the source of the disturbance, and my right arm and shoulder became cold. I felt a strange vibrating energy move INTO my right shoulder, pass through my neck and chest, and exit my body through my left shoulder. I could still feel the cold spot next to me on my left side, lasting about five seconds. I stood in silent shock for several moments, and then I asked out loud, "Did someone just walk THROUGH me?!" I didn't receive an answer...not one that I detected at the time, anyway. Nora did add that Indian Charlie liked to walk back and forth in front of the bar. We finished the setup of the equipment, and then I sat through both ghost tours hosted that night, enjoying the incredible verbal interactions and flashlight activations, but I was also recording the tours with my night-vision camera for more documentary footage.

The working weekend of ghost tours and video footage came to an end, and my family returned to my parents' house, as I had to catch a plane back to my home the next morning. Many members of my extended family stopped by to visit me before I left. After dinner, we moved into the long living room, and the ghost tours and evidence we collected in Tombstone were the hot topics of conversation. My family has been very supportive of this journey I am on, and they continued to ask me about my interactions and sensitivity. I was sitting on one end of a comfortable loveseat, and my attention was all over the place. On one side of the room, I was talking to my cousin and her husband about some of the things that he has experienced, and I was providing him some feedback on how he should study what he went through. At the same time, I was talking with my sister's husband and my mother on the other side of the room about the strange shadow figure and the sensation of that energy flowing through me right in front of the bar. My sister was sitting next to me on the loveseat, with her head on my shoulder, and with my left hand, I was directly some Reiki healing energy to help soothe her discomfort. My intention and sensitivity was directed all around the room. It was relaxing for me, and it was great to share so much of my energy to help my family. When it was time to go, everyone started to stand up and say their "goodbyes" to each other...everyone except me. I was totally distracted, and everyone was wondering why I was staring down at my right hand.

Before I could stand up, I suddenly felt my right hand begin to hum with energy, as if the nerves and muscles in my hand were vibrating. My hand also started growing warmer, until my hand, forearm, and elbow felt feverish with heat; the skin on my arm was actually flushed with the energy. Soon after, my left hand also heated up with intense energy. I instinctively knew that I was supposed to do something with this building metaphysical energy, but I didn't know what. I announced to the room that my hands were vibrating and exceedingly hot with energy, and the conversations went quiet. I started to look around the room to see what I was supposed to do next. I looked over at my cousin, reading her body energy and seeing some of the pain in her neck and shoulders. I stood up and walked over to give her a hug, and she said, "Please don't hurt me..." I laughed and jokingly scolded her: "C'mere! I'm not gonna hurt you, sheesh!" When I wrapped my arms around her, I received intuitive messages that told me she wasn't the intended release point. Aloud I said, "Hmm, nooooo..." I turned to my right, and my somewhat hazy gaze passed on to my sister. I evaluated her energy levels as well, but no, she wasn't the energy outlet, either, and this energy was starting to make my fingers tremble. By this time, everyone in the room was watching me intently, but I was only half-aware of their gazes. I cast my sensitivity around the room, but nothing in the room responded in a way that I could detect. I looked down at the floor for a moment, and an unexpected image entered my head: an old sketch from the late 1800s of a man with features of mixed descent. I had seen this picture before; it was a sketch of Indian Charlie. As soon as I recognized it, the entire sketch flashed with bright light in my vision. HE was the one with whom this energy should be used?! I said out loud, "You gotta be KIDDING me..." Suddenly, my senses were blotted out with shimmering white light. A second later, my consciousness was standing back in the Tombstone mortuary! My hands were both on top of the bar, and immediately, two black, viscous shadow hands moved to lay themselves on top of mine in this vision. I couldn't make out any distinguishing features on the hands, but I could see the semi-solid forms of each individual finger. I lifted my head slowly. I could also see that the two shadow hands led up to this shadow figure's wrists and forearms, but beyond that, the two arms were reaching out of a large black shadow mass of no discernable shape. I could feel the humming touch of the entity's fingertips and the unnaturally light weight of the hands themselves. I KNEW this energy; there was no mistaking its source. The pent-up energy in my fingers began to drain into the shadow fingers that held the backs of my hands. Without knowing why, I looked over my left shoulder in this vision while these shadow hands were still covering mine. I could see that Nora was in this vision. She and I locked eyes for a long moment, and she seemed to recognize me, and then my vision of the mortuary went dark. My consciousness came back to the living room, and I was on my feet with an expression of utter surprise.

Before I could commit any words to what had just happened, my extra-sensory perception received an inspiring explanation. I started babbling in my excitement: "Ohmygodohmygodohmygod..." Everyone in the room was asking me if I was all right after seeing the change in my expression. My mother asked me, "What is it? What just happened?" I told her to wait a moment, and I choose to make my announcement to my cousin and her husband first: "I think I just projected my energy to Tombstone to interact with Indian Charlie! Ohmygod, ohmygod..." It was the EXACT energy, in frequency and intensity, that I had felt when the energy of that entity passed through me in front of the bar two days earlier! Every instinct told me it had really happened. My intuitive messages confirmed that it was not Indian Charlie coming to my parents' home; I had projected my consciousness to Tombstone in this remote viewing event. I was overwhelmed. I kept walking around the house describing what I had seen, and soon I had problems talking: my teeth were chattering like crazy, and I was shivering with the personal drain I felt after the energy dissipation. (Keep in mind, this was Arizona in May. There was no natural reason for why my teeth should be chattering...) This was the most incredible experience I had had to date...and I couldn't figure out how I actually accomplished it! When I finally calmed down fifteen minutes later, I sat back down, feeling very drained. After my cousin left, the remaining family members and I started to talk excitedly about all of the paranormal events that took place that weekend leading up to this distance projection of my sensitivity.

The discussions were free-flowing, and we jumped around through a variety of subjects. Some were about different intuitive visions I had during Reiki sessions, and others were revisiting different sights and sounds from the ghost tours across the previous months. The experiences I shared continued to amaze me, especially since my "awakening" with Reiki took place only about six months earlier. My mother shared a recurring theme about my sensitivity evolving "as it was meant to be," as if there was some higher purpose and design for my efforts. While many people may agree with this, I've always had an issue with accepting these kinds of statements, because I am firmly grounded in the belief that I drive my own fate. My decisions, my initiative, and my proactive planning dictate the events around me that I can control; in my mind, my personal path isn't decided by Fate. I've lived my life with my own self-reliance and my deep self-awareness, and I will continue to do so. I am proud of my accomplishments. I don't get annoyed or upset when talking about the possibility of a higher purpose driving my spiritual journey; it's simply not how I view things. When the discussion came back to the mind-blowing consciousness projection I experienced with Indian Charlie only a few hours earlier, I still couldn't figure out how I did it. How was I able to send my awareness...to...right at this point in my thought, I had what I would have to call an overwhelming epiphany, and my mind and spirit reeled together at the ramifications of my realization.

To me, my sensitivity has come from my journey through the eye of a paradox: my free will and drive IS part of the grand scheme in store for me! As different as these perspectives may sound, they are not mutually exclusive; there is a point at which both can be true, and that is the paradox in which I have found my sensitivity. My self-initiative and my personal control of my destiny can BE the instruments to achieve what is meant to me. My work and training, my testing, my analysis...why CAN'T they be contributing to things happening when they are supposed to happen, as determined by Fate or a higher power? This would certainly show me that I am on the "right path" in my evolution. All of these thoughts just flooded into my head in rapid succession, and I saw the Panther's face appear next to me, over my right shoulder, to say, "Thank God! FINALLY!!" I couldn't help but laugh at his mock exasperation. It was an effective confirmation, though; the Panther was waiting for me to make this realization on my own, so that I had a new way forward to address some of these self-imposed challenges that my own viewpoints were causing.

It totally changed my perspective from pursuing things to see *if* I can learn to expand my abilities to investigating new techniques and theories and waiting for *when* I will learn new ways to use this gift. It also made me rethink how I keep telling people that anyone can perform Reiki, because the main "skill" required is the intention to heal someone. Reflecting on my engineering studies related to the conservation of energy, why can't anyone learn to identify paranormal energies as well? There are many common practices between them, so it seems logical.

And then I had Epiphany #2. (This was a busy night of discoveries for me!) This new thought addressed another self-defined paradox I had struggled with, and I finally resolved it. The acceptance of my first paradox enabled the re-evaluation of my struggles between my analytical self and these new-found energy sensitivities that I can't explain. My logical mind does NOT have to be separate from the extra-sensory perceptions of Reiki and my interactions with the paranormal. My belief focuses on the INTENTION, which has always been the key to self-reliance and deciding my own fate, and my perception accepts the results of the intending healing. Add the sensitivity to the paranormal to this explanation, and my self-initiative has simply expanded my intention to detect new levels of energy. Accepting this paradox was harder, since it was still based upon the evaluating the results of my sensitivity against my extensive imagination in order to verify the experiences were coming from "outside" of me. I found myself walking in the eye of not one but TWO paradoxes in the way I defined myself on this evolutionary journey. Talk about enlightenment! There will be people who will say, "Of COURSE they are related! How could you do one without the other?" To that, I will simply say, "Remember, knowing the path is very different from walking the path." It was an evening of revelations for me, ones that I needed yet weren't previously pursuing on my own. In good conscience, I have to ask myself, "Were these discussions meant to be?" They lasted into the early hours of the morning, until I was finally exhausted and had to get some sleep.

But before I went to sleep, I decided to try and corroborate my impressions and visions I had during this projection of consciousness with the one person I saw experiencing it with me. I sent a rather generic e-mail to Nora, and I told her that "something unusual" had happened that day, without specifying a time. I asked her if she has sensed anything related to me in the mortuary at any point. I purposely omitted any reference to my contact with Indian Charlie or my location in front of the bar. I didn't even say I saw her in my remote viewing experience. The next morning, I traveled to the airport and was checking my personal email while waiting to board when I noticed Nora that had already responded to me. Nora told me that, yes, she has sensed my energy around 8:15 pm in the mortuary's bar area. According to her account, I was standing in front of the bar, and she knew it was me. She felt her hands heat up to "130 degrees" when she sensed my presence; I never told her about how my hands and arms became unnaturally warm. She even matched the time of the event - I couldn't believe it! I puzzled over her story for days, and I couldn't come up with any other explanation except that the spiritual "trip" I took over 200 miles actually took place! Let me tell you: that was one hell of a night...and I believe I have only scratched the surface of this thing. I couldn't find another logical explanation for all of this, so it was time to really dig into the Declaration.

By the way, that wasn't the only time that Indian Charlie and I interacted remotely. For some reason, he seems to be connected to me after our encounter in Tombstone, and he is adept at spirit travel. I was home one night, jogging on my treadmill and watching TV, when I felt a strange tingling and dizziness. By now, I had figured out the meaning behind these signs, and I immediately put up my psychic shield. I had never seen nor experienced any paranormal phenomena in my house before this night, so it was a surprise that I would begin to sense something while on the treadmill. I shifted my perception away from the TV program and "listened" to the intuitive thoughts appearing at the edge of my senses. I started to talk out loud in a stream of consciousness in response to the messages until I identified the source. When a cold spot touched my shoulder, I immediately associated the latent energy with my "friend" Indian Charlie. At the corner of my inner sight, I saw a shadow figure with two white pinholes as eyes looking at me. The figure didn't say a word, but there was no need. I acknowledged him mentally, but I spoke verbally to tell him he was not allowed to come visit me in my house without my invitation. It was not an appropriate use of our "connection," and I promised to come see him soon back in Tombstone. The shadow figure vanished, all traces of the disorientation and the cold energy disappearing along with him. I am looking forward to our next meeting.

After a little over a year, I have gone through amazement, frustration, confusion, and enlightenment, the likes of which I have never experienced before. My life has been forever changed in a very short time, and I'm still learning ways in which my views of the world, and other worlds I am discovering, are being altered. "Reiki healer" and "paranormal sensitive" are two titles that I never predicted to give myself, yet I haven't found any more appropriate ways to describe my current states in this spiritual evolution. Even my recounting all of these experiences in this book has had a purpose for me: it has re-energized my excitement to continue my exploration of these new connections. If you have made it this far into my story, then I'd say it is safe to assume that you have found some type of appreciation for the events, visions, stories, or even my internal dialogue that I have shared; hopefully, it's all of the above. But why do you think that is? For those of you who know me, you know how committed I am to this, but it's not just the incredible phenomena I describe that have convinced you of my commitment. My hope is that it is the fact that I can convey the depths of my powerful commitment in "spite" of my logical, practical, experimental personality that most people would assume contradict the belief in these metaphysical and paranormal events. Actually, I have found out how to unite my engineering mind with my metaphysical gifts, and in doing so, I have enriched both. Looking at the struggles I have gone through in order to embrace this spiritual enlightenment, I still shake my head at what I faced. Then again, look at what I accomplished by fighting through the challenges. If I can put aside my preconceived notions, anyone can. I truly believe that it takes one simple step to direct your life in a new, gratifying direction. If you have experienced a connection with my journey of spiritual growth, then I've accomplished what I set out to do in this book.

From a technical standpoint, there are parallels that can be drawn between energy sensitivity and the evolution of technology to expand our knowledge of the world around us. For example, there are many technologies that have helped move paranormal research forward. With the theories that spirits can utilize the energy around them to help them manifest and communicate, cold spots and static charges are often believed to be indicators of paranormal activity. There are many devices, like digital thermometers and electromagnetic field detectors, that are employed to detect the presence of these events. Before the invention of these devices, all of the scales of measurement for these phenomena were based upon how a person interacted with them, until someone determined an effective technical process to create an agreed-upon measurement tool to define the phenomenon. Even the visible spectrum of the human eye has been "expanded" through the development of infrared, ultraviolet, and thermal imaging devices. We couldn't see into these spectrums in the past, yet these technologies evolved to incorporate these new events into our views of the natural world, and now they are often used when investigating many metaphysical energy events. If we are able to find ways to interact with these energy phenomena after identifying their physical characteristics, it seems possible that we can also train ourselves to sense the same energy fluctuations and frequencies once we know what to look for. Patience and attention to detail will go far in identifying these energies. The first step is to try.

Intention is the key that can unlock many doors. Think about the impact of simply willing another person, or yourself, to have improved health and less emotional stress. All it takes is your intention to direct your thoughts toward helping another human being feel better. If all you show them is a good night's sleep, it is rewarding, but you can't always foresee just how big of an impact your actions may have in the future. A few weeks after a Reiki session I performed on a friend, we got together for a few drinks. At the time, my sensitivity was an all-consuming topic for me, so I shared a lot of my recent insights and visions over dinner. My friend was supportive and interested, so we talked about all sorts of things. My friend then paused for a moment, looking down at the table, and then looked at me, saying, "Thank you. I have to tell you that you taught me something. You helped me to forgive." Finding forgiveness for a person who has wronged you is a hard-enough prospect, but the next statement was my favorite: "And I am starting to forgive myself." I was so proud! What an amazing step toward some type of inner peace! With that first attempt at shedding negative emotional energy you put upon yourself, you've started down the road of actively working to heal your own wounds. This was one of the best rewards I've ever received for my Reiki efforts.

I can go on and on, describing how my steps on this journey have affected family, friends, and even strangers, and I could use their own words of praise and wonder. I can describe the sincere gratification I have felt by helping people to find a little peace and telling them what I have experienced, regardless of the belief or skepticism I receive in response. One of the most moving feelings I have ever had is through showing people that the sadness and pain they are experiencing at that time are not the sum total of their lives; showing a person that he or she has experienced peace and strength before, and can do so again, resonates within me. However, I would like to reiterate that my self-initiative drives my Reiki energy work as well as my spirit mediumship. Simply put, Reiki is the direction of healing energy into others. What's the worst thing that could happen when using Reiki? Nothing. What's the best thing that can happen? A miracle. Who knows what else you may find you are capable of? It has been an infinitely worthwhile pursuit for me, even though I have to deal with an enormous black panther with a sarcastic wit and a faceless Jesuit monk to keep me on the right path. It's a path of enlightenment that I am proud of. Maybe it's time for you to take stock of your own spiritual evolution; if this appeals to you, go for it. You won't regret it.

There have been other personal rewards I have been "given" as I've traveled down this completely unanticipated path of sensitivity. Considering the nature of energy exchange and conservation, I'm kind of surprised it didn't occur to me before, but some things you have to experience for yourself in order to understand them. This is often true for both Reiki healers and their clients. I've spent a lot of time telling people about the incredible visions I have received during sessions, and I continue to protect the privacy of the people who trusted me enough to ask me for my Reiki healing. One woman who had heard many of my stories finally opted to have a reading of her own. At the beginning of the session, she couldn't stop giggling nervously, having no idea how it would feel to her while I was guiding universal energy into her. She informed me that she could actually feel a tingling sensation when I worked to reduce the pain in her left knee, and I could see a red cord of negative energy leading up from her knee to her lower back. Working to draw this swelling out of her, I received a vision of her as a little girl of age 6. She was standing outside in a sundress with vertical stripes on it, and she wasn't wearing any shoes. (At this description, she burst out laughing, "That's GOT to be me!") The scene unfolded as she was yelling at her older sister. She was furious with her sister because her sister had betrayed her trust, and then her father appeared in the vision. Her father was very disappointed in the little girl, but the intuitive messages informed me that it wasn't her fault. I completed the Reiki session, and the woman was almost asleep. She claimed that she could still feel the energy and tingling in her feet where I had pulled out the negative energy from her chakras. With my attunement to her energy, I tapped into the emotional pain she experienced, and she was able to feel the draining of emotional negativity. Her knee felt tickling sensations, her feet felt tingling, and her throat become very warm...yet I was at least two feet away from her during the entire session. Using my analogy of my ability to adapt my energy, in form and frequency, to read my subject's physical and emotional states, this leads me to a new insight: I have to think that we are all connected in some way if we can actually attune ourselves to each other. If we can connect with each other's energy, not one of us is really ever alone, is he? One connection leads to another, and then another, yet the basis is the same. A connection with another person, living or after death, all starts with one small step: intention.

Notes

[1] The Burlington County Prison Museum is located at 128 High Street, Mount Holly, New Jersey, USA.

[2] National Aeronautics and Space Administration, *Newton's Laws of Motion*, http://www.grc.nasa.gov/WWW/k-12/airplane/newton.html.

[3] National Aeronautics and Space Administration, *The Lift Equation*, http://www.grc.nasa.gov/WWW/K-12/airplane/lifteq.html.

[4] Encyclopaedia Brittanica, *E=mc²*, http://www.britannica.com/EBchecked/topic/1666493/E-mc2.

[5] Wikipedia Encyclopaedia, *Theory of Relativity*, http://en.wikipedia.org/wiki/Theory_of_relativity.

[6] The "Watt & Tarbell, Undertakers" mortuary is located at 521 East Allen Street, Tombstone, Arizona, USA.

[7] Sister Paranormal Investigators are registered on Facebook. http://www.facebook.com/SisterParanormalInvestigators?fref=ts

[8] Wilde, Stuart, *Sixth Sense*, (2000), Hay House, USA.

[9] The Nuffield Foundation, *Practical Physics: The law of conservation of energy*, http://www.nuffieldfoundation.org/node/1842.

[10] The Eastern State Penitentiary is located at 2027 Fairmont Avenue, Philadelphia, Pennsylvania, USA.

[11] Correspondence with Lee Van Zyl, Reiki Northeast, Montclair Metaphysical & Healing Center, 16 Park Avenue, Rutherford, New Jersey, USA. http://www.montclairmetaphysical.com/reiki-north-east.

[12] The Merchants' House Museum is located at 29 East Fourth Street, New York, New York, USA.

Made in the USA
Middletown, DE
02 October 2015